Privatizing Public Enterprises

The RIPA, founded in 1922, is the leading independent British institution concerned with policy-making and administration in the public sector. Its aims are to help improve the effectiveness of public administration and to increase public understanding of institutions, processes and policies in the public service. It is concerned both with the needs of public authorities and also with the needs of the public they serve.

Privatizing Public Enterprises: Options and Dilemmas

Edited by
David Steel and David Heald

ROYAL INSTITUTE OF PUBLIC ADMINISTRATION

First published in 1984

The contents of this book represent the views of the authors alone and in no way commit the organizations of which they are members. The contents have not been considered by the Council of the RIPA and do not necessarily reflect the views of the Council or of the members of the RIPA.

Published by the Royal Institute of Public Administration,
3 Birdcage Walk, London SW1H 9JH.

Printed in England by Victoria House Printing Co.,
124/130 Tabernacle Street, London EC2

ISBN 0 900628 35 9

Contents

Acknowledgements

This volume consists of revised versions of papers which were originally presented to a research workshop on 'The Privatization of Public Enterprises', which was held on 26-28 April 1984 at the University of Exeter's Crossmead Conference Centre. It was the third of a series of small workshops organized under the auspices of the Public Administration Committee of the Joint University Council for Social and Public Administration. The seminar was made possible through grants from the Joint University Council itself, the Nuffield Foundation and the University of Exeter. It was organized by David Steel and David Heald who are the joint conveners of the Royal Institute of Public Administration's Research Group on Public Enterprise.

Contributors

David Heald is Lecturer in Management Studies at the University of Glasgow where he specializes in finance and public sector management. He is the author of *Public Expenditure: Its Defence and Reform* (Martin Robertson 1983) and has written extensively on privatization in collaboration with David Steel. Also a qualified accountant, with experience of both the public and private sectors, he has acted as specialist adviser to the Treasury and Civil Service Committee and the Committee on Scottish Affairs.

John Kay is Director of the Institute for Fiscal Studies and a Fellow of St. John's College, Oxford. He is co-author (with Leslie Hannah) of *Concentration in Modern Industry* (Macmillan 1977) and (with Mervyn King) of *The British Tax System* (Oxford University Press 1983). The author of many academic articles, he has also edited a number of economic journals, including the IFS house journal, *Fiscal Studies,* which he founded. He has acted as specialist adviser to the Treasury and Civil Service Committee and as consultant to private firms in the UK and for government and international bodies in other countries.

Craig Pickering is Lecturer in Public Sector Management at the London Business School. After completing a political science doctorate in totalitarianism at London University, he taught and then joined the Treasury as an administrator, holding posts in nationalized industry financial control and in the private offices of two permanent secretaries. In 1983 he left the civil service to join the London Business School where he is conducting research on privatization.

David Steel was until July 1984 Lecturer in Politics at the University of Exeter where he specialized in public administration. Since completing a doctoral thesis at Nuffield College on the British Transport Commission, he has written extensively on the nationalized industries and central government. He is the co-author (with the late Ronald Brown) of *The Administrative Process in Britain* (Methuen 1979). With David Heald, he has been researching and publishing on various dimensions of this Government's programme for privatizing public enterprises.

David Thomas is the Industrial Correspondent of *New Society.* Before becoming a journalist, he was Assistant Secretary (Public Industry) in the Economic Department of the Trades Union Congress. In that capacity, he helped service a number of committees responsible for the TUC's work on the nationalized industries and helped advise the TUC representatives on the NEDO working parties on nationalized industries' investment and energy prices. His Cambridge doctorate has been published as *Naturalism and Social Science* (Cambridge University Press 1980).

Michael Webb is a Senior Research Fellow at the Oxford Institute for Energy Studies and Fellow of St. Antony's College, Oxford. He has written extensively on investment and pricing in the nationalized industries, particularly in the energy sector, and is author of *The Economics of Nationalised Industries* (Nelson 1973), *Pricing Policies for Public Enterprises* (Macmillan 1976) and (with Martin Ricketts) *The Economics of Energy* (Macmillan 1980). He also has wide practical experience as a consultant on, for example, World Bank and Asian Development Bank projects, and has recently returned to academic life after a period in full-time consultancy.

Seminar Participants

Christopher Beauman	Morgan Grenfell
Peter Gist	London Business School
Gerry Grimstone	HM Treasury
Graham Houston	HM Treasury
Robert Millward	University of Salford
Jeremy Moon	University of Strathclyde
Peter Moulson	Cable & Wireless
Douglas Pitt	University of Strathclyde
John Rhys	Electricity Council
Jeffery Wheatley	British Telecommunications

Abbreviations

ENTERPRISE

ABP	Associated British Ports
AI	Amersham International
BA	British Airways
BAA	British Airports Authority
BAe	British Aerospace
BGC	British Gas Corporation
BL	British Leyland
BNFL	British Nuclear Fuels
BNOC	British National Oil Corporation
BP	British Petroleum
BR	British Rail
BS	British Shipbuilders
BSC	British Steel Corporation
BT	British Telecommunications
BTDB	British Transport Docks Board
CAA	Civil Aviation Authority
C&W	Cable & Wireless
CEGB	Central Electricity Generating Board
ESI	Electricity Supply Industry
NBC	National Bus Company
NCB	National Coal Board
NEB	National Enterprise Board
NFC	National Freight Corporation/Company/Consortium
PO	Post Office
ROFs	Royal Ordnance Factories
RR	Rolls-Royce
UKAEA	United Kingdom Atomic Energy Authority

UNION

APEX	Association of Professional, Executive, Clerical and Computer Staff
ASTMS	Association of Scientific, Technical and Managerial Staffs
AUEW-TASS	Amalgamated Union of Engineering Workers (Technical, Administrative and Supervisory Section)
BACM	British Association of Colliery Management
BTUC	British Telecommunications Union Committee
CPSA	Civil and Public Services Association
CSEU	Confederation of Shipbuilding and Engineering Unions
EMA	Engineers' and Managers' Association
ISTC	Iron and Steel Trades Confederation
MNAOA	Merchant Navy and Airline Officers' Association
NALGO	National and Local Government Officers' Association
NUM	National Union of Mineworkers

NUR	National Union of Railwaymen
POEU	Post Office Engineering Union
SIMA	Steel Industry Management Association
STE	Society of Telecommunications Executives
TGWU	Transport and General Workers' Union
TSSA	Transport Salaried Staffs' Association
TUC	Trades Union Congress
UCW	Union of Communication Workers
URTU	United Road Transport Union

OTHER

AGR	Advanced Gas-cooled Reactor
BST	Bulk Supply Tariff
CBI	Confederation of British Industry
CPRS	Central Policy Review Staff
CSO	Central Statistical Office
DCF	Discounted Cash Flow
EFL	External Financing Limit
IBA	Independent Broadcasting Authority
LRMC	Long Run Marginal Cost
MMC	Monopolies and Mergers Commission
MW	Megawatt
NATO	North Atlantic Treaty Organization
NEDC	National Economic Development Council
NEDO	National Economic Development Office
NHS	National Health Service
NICG	Nationalised Industries' Chairmen's Group
OECD	Organization for Economic Co-operation and Development
OFTEL	Office of Telecommunications
PAC	Public Accounts Committee
PESC	Public Expenditure Survey (Committee)
PLP	Parliamentary Labour Party
PSBR	Public Sector Borrowing Requirement
RRR	Required Rate of Return

Preface
Alastair Morton

The present Government is determined, *inter alia*, to remove a variety of assets and undertakings from the public to the private sector. However, the delays during Mrs Thatcher's first Administration make it necessary to press on now, risking occasional snafus. Now, there should be no question in any intelligent mind that our governments *must* keep under review the boundary between the public and private sectors. Why, for example, should the taxpayer own and support, seek or decline to profit from, this or that business? There is a category of asset — British Transport Hotels, for example — that has no business in the taxpayers' hands. There is also a category for which the public interest may be as well served by a regulated, private sector monopoly as a public sector monopoly — telecommunications and airways, for example.

But as one continues down the list, one sees the categories where the public or national interest will often create policy/profit dilemmas for a business — Cable & Wireless and the Royal Ordnance Factories, for example — and the categories which must compete commercially in their markets but currently cannot for some reason — British Steel. And so on, initiating many policy questions.

'*Can* we privatize X Corporation?' is a question that melds rather quickly into '*Why* are we trying to privatize X?' The widely and justifiably-held suspicion that the Treasury, so powerful in this area, is in it for this year's proceeds — for the loot — soon confuses the discussion. The fact that ministers and mandarins worship an unsubstantiable effigy called PSBR and thus sell the State's capital furnishings to pay for current wages and benefits sheds more heat than light upon the issues.

Because issues there are. To name but one, Britain does not have a well-constituted policy of regulation and it is hard to generate one in an atmosphere of deregulation. For a second issue, consider the cross-subsidy arguments generated by a profitable subsidiary (e.g. Jaguar) within a struggling, public sector group (British Leyland), or an unprofitable airliner within a successful, privatized British Aerospace. For a third, there are the pricing decisions for the gas and telecommunications monopolies, soon to be in different sectors. Overall, there is the intellectual and professional disorder in public accounting and funding.

The more cogent the policy dialogue on privatization, the more hope we have of avoiding the perils of a 'ready, shoot, aim' sequence in the Government's approach to privatization in the three years probably remaining of Mrs Thatcher's second administration. It is analysis and purposeful preparation we need, not rhetoric. Ministers and other commentators do no good at all by slashing attacks, for example, on management inefficiency in the public sector — that demoralizes exceptionally hardworking people and is demonstrably untrue in several easy to cite cases. Both the enterprises that move into the private sector and the great industrial and service concerns that inevitably remain in the public sector must be managed by good teams, not placemen. It is ministers' difficult enough task to put them in place. Further, both hybrids and public sector corporations must have clear definitions of their future relationship with public finances — a debate that can only grow more acute when revenues from North Sea oil decline, not long after Mrs Thatcher's privatizing second administration.

I am encouraged by the work of the editors and the RIPA to develop an intelligent policy dialogue, involving Treasury officials, informed academics, the City and industry. The workshop that generated these chapters was a milestone in an urgent journey. Unless we make that journey into the policy issues *now* we may find some cases of privatization are neither effective nor efficient, and cannot continue long-term. It is unnecessary but perfectly possible that this will happen; and if it does then the 'British decline' will be reinforced instead of reversed by some of the Government's initiatives in this area.

Alastair Morton is Chief Executive of a City banking and financial services group. His board level public sector experience from 1968 to 1980 embraced industrial reorganization, nuclear power, hospitals, armaments, steel and oil. He was guest speaker at the workshop at which the chapters in this book were originally delivered.

1

The New Agenda

David Steel and David Heald

In February 1980, the editors of this book presented a paper to the inaugural meeting of the Royal Institute of Public Administration's Research Group on Public Enterprise (later published as Heald and Steel 1981) on the then recently elected Conservative Government's programme for privatizing public enterprises. On that occasion, part of the audience accused them of making a mountain out of a molehill on the grounds that the programme was destined to peter out once ministers came face to face with the realities of office. That judgement could not have been proved more wrong. 'Privatization' is rapidly becoming the dominant political issue of the decade. It has taken many forms and guises, all of which reflect a political commitment to 'roll back the public sector' and to 'free market forces'. However, as a policy prescription or description, it has come to embrace too many distinct instruments and actions to be a sufficiently well-defined term of analysis. It is therefore essential to identify the major components and to recognize both their distinctiveness and interactions.

Privatization has four main components (Heald 1983, 1984). *Charging* involves the (partial) substitution of user charges for tax finance. *Contracting-out* represents the substitution of private contractors for in-house production. *Denationalization and load-shedding* refer to reductions in the scope of public sector activity, taking the forms, respectively, of the sale of public enterprises and the (partial) abandonment of public non-market functions. Liberalization means the removal of statutory prohibitions on the private sector competing against the public sector. The scope and variation in the policy measures covered by the term are immediately apparent. This book, like the Workshop on which it is based, has a carefully specified and restricted remit. Its concern is with public enterprises, with the result that it is only the implementation of policies of denationalization and liberalization which is explored.

Even after this narrowing, the scale, diversity and complexity of the policy issues remain formidable. Without question, Mrs Thatcher's Government will be remembered as the most radical administration since the post-war

Labour Government in terms of its impact upon the nature and size of the public sector of industry. This judgement would hold simply in terms of the changes implemented during its first term (Steel and Heald, forthcoming). Taking denationalization alone, BAe, C&W, AI, Britoil and ABP[1] are an impressive start, making the Heath Government's record (the sale of two travel agents and the state management districts which was more than offset by the nationalization of RR) look derisory in comparison. Moreover, the Government's commitment to privatization has gathered momentum rather than weakened and much of the groundwork undertaken in the early years of the programme will bear fruit during the Government's second term.

The Conservative Party's 1979 manifesto provided no hint of the way in which privatization was to become a central theme of Mrs Thatcher's Government. The only glimmer as to future developments was the Ridley Report of 1978, leaked at the time (*The Economist* 1978) and still unpublished, but providing an agenda for taming the nationalized sector. Should Mrs Thatcher secure a third term, this document, judging by the leaked summary, will look prophetic. The programme also survived the inevitable period of gestation associated with parliamentary proceedings on the first bills and the background preparatory work, when it was easy for sympathisers to complain, and critics to sneer, that it was all talk and little action. Speeches by Sir Geoffrey Howe in July 1981 (Howe 1981) and Mr John Moore in November 1983 (Moore 1983) were significant public landmarks in the evolution and defence of the programme.

Moreover, privatization fits in neatly with Mrs Thatcher's style of 'conviction politics'. Most post-war governments, when faced by political and economic crises, have trimmed their ideological and manifesto commitments so as to lay claim to what they saw as the middle ground. Instead, Mrs Thatcher's style under pressure has been to re-emphasize ideological commitment and to shift and restructure the political spectrum. In the difficult days of 1981, the privatization of nationalized industries functioned as a unifying mechanism for a Conservative Party deeply divided over macroeconomic policy: hostility towards the sector spreads right across the Conservative benches. The commitment held firm until the first legislative measures matured into implementation, with the successful transfer of the first crop of enterprises into the private sector. Then, the confidence and expectation of another term generated by the Falklands War played their part in stimulating development work on later crops. Now, the most likely response to assorted 'banana skins', including those directly related to the privatization programme such as the Enterprise Oil flotation (which occurred after the chapters of this book had been finalized), will be for the Government to accelerate its pace (see Moore 1984).

Although the programme will not be completed by the end of its second term, the Government will nonetheless have fashioned a truly 'irreversible shift'. Even if the political pendulum were to swing decisively in the opposite direction during the late 1980s, it is inconceivable that current policies will not be seen as a major landmark. Decisions taken now may unleash new opportunities but they will also close options by the new structure of interests which they create. Should a future government wish to reverse privatization, it is unlikely that it would be able, even if it so wished, to restore the status quo ante. Not least, the financial costs of renationalization might be seen as prohibitive even by a left-wing Labour Government, especially when set against its expenditure priorities in the social field. The present Government's programme to date has certainly demonstrated that, in budgetary terms at least, denationalization is much easier to implement than nationalization. In part, but only in part, this affords support to Sir Geoffrey Howe's surprise (Howe 1981) that earlier Conservative Governments had never unwound the nationalization measures which they had vigorously denounced in opposition.

The more fundamental point, however, relates to the dramatic change in the intellectual and political climate towards the public sector, and the way in which the radicalization of the Conservative Party during the 1974-79 spell in opposition has enabled it to harness this changed mood. Undeniably, the Government's twin themes of rolling back the public sector and restricting the power of the trade unions have struck favourable chords with the electorate. Although the arguments are rarely articulated in this way, the privatization of public enterprises has been seen by the Government as contributing towards four objectives: it will enhance freedom by extending the sphere of the market and contracting that of the state; it will improve efficiency because private sector organizations are inherently more efficient than public ones; it will reduce the PSBR; and it will re-introduce market disciplines missing in the determination of public sector pay (Heald and Steel 1982).

What is striking about the manner in which these arguments are deployed by ministers is that they are rarely hedged by qualifications. *If* these propositions about freedom and efficiency are accepted, every extension of privatization is desirable. There is no requirement for careful balancing of the merits of public and private ownership or of the scope and desirability of competition on a case-by-case basis. The injunction is the antithesis of a literal reading of Clause IV (4) of the Labour Party's constitution which leaves no scope for private ownership in industry. Privatization thus has few obvious logical bounds until the economic and social activities of the state have been drastically reduced from their present scope. In particular, there is, on such presumptions, no logical reason to restrict privatization to the public market sector and to leave the public non-market sector largely untouched. *If* public ownership is so destructive of freedom and efficiency that it is impossible through financial control and the injection of competition to run industries efficiently whilst they remain in the public sector, must these defects not also apply to the budget-financed (virtual) monopolies in health and education? There may be questions about what the electorate will now accept, and about the practical constraints on the speed of implementation, but these are matters of tactics, hardly of principle. The conflict within the Conservative Party about the future of public spending and the welfare state is thus between those who see privatization as relevant and essential throughout the public sector and those who wish to restrict its domain primarily to the nationalized industries.

Perhaps the most surprising aspect of the programme to date, and one which has undoubtedly stimulated its evolution and extension, has been the feebleness of the opposition mounted against such an ambitious set of changes. Incapacitated by internal conflict over its own constitution, the Labour Party has singularly failed either to articulate a coherent defence of the principle of public ownership or to mount an effective campaign against the gradual but systematic dismantling of an important part of the legacy of 1945. In part, its efforts have been distracted by the tension between the strong ideological commitment of party activists outside Parliament to public ownership as a matter of socialist principle and the electorate's hostility both to further nationalization and to the existing nationalized industries. Whilst that wider public opinion was unlikely to be convinced by appeal to abstract principle, it might have been persuaded in specific cases had the pragmatic arguments been effectively marshalled within the context of a cogent defence of continued public ownership in particular sectors. To do this, the Party would have had to clarify its attitude towards liberalization, as distinct from denationalization, especially in sectors facing rapid technological changes, on which it (if not necessarily the trade unions) could have readily conceded ground without sacrificing principle. Blanket opposition to a programme as pervasive as privatization inevitably blunts the effectiveness and impact of specific objections. Whether or not the Government has enjoyed public support for a programme far exceeding its original manifesto 'mandate', the Labour Party ought to be desperately worried that such far-reaching changes could be implemented without producing much public reaction, with boredom more evident than anger. This is all the more surprising given two critical reports from the PAC (1982, 1984) which have raised serious doubts about the conduct of the sales.

Few voices have been raised in defence of the nationalized industries. With a limited number of exceptions, the union response has been one of reluctant acquiescence. Confronted by high unemployment and a succession of restrictive labour legislation, the unions' troubles have been manifold. In the absence of seething mass political discontent, there has been little that they could do other than to engage in damage limitation as regards pay and conditions. Moreover, opposition to privatization led by public sector trade unions has resulted in a degree of public scepticism about their motives, skilfully exploited by ministerial attacks upon both industrial relations records and 'excessive' pay and conditions. Perhaps most interesting of all has been the attitude of the nationalized industries themselves. The NICG has stood aside in the course of the privatization

Defence? NI's

debates and, in public at least, has left its member industries to fight their own corners. Few of them have been inclined to assert publicly the benefits of continued public ownership, taking the view that this is a matter for Parliament to decide. It is not known what they said privately to ministers and departments about the principle of denationalization but it is obvious from subsequent events that they successfully resisted having their main businesses broken up prior to sale (BAe, ABP and BT but interestingly not BL). Increasingly, one of the difficulties of running a nationalized industry has been the adverse image of the sector, with most of its members being caricatured either as chronically inefficient loss-makers or as consumer-exploiting monopolies. The problems and failings of individual enterprises have had far-reaching consequences, tarnishing the reputations of others even though they are connected only by the fact of public ownership.

Confronted by the Government's generalized commitment to privatization, nationalized industry management has faced a dilemma. The ministers charged with their supervision, both at the Treasury and at the sponsoring departments, have often seemed more concerned to attack the industries' records, as proof of the folly of public ownership, than to confront strategic business issues. If the composer and conductor have lost faith in the score, that leaves the orchestra in a quandary. In the first two years of the Government, the nationalized industries became visibly upset by the Treasury's enforcement of restrictive EFLs. These were at odds with corporate plans and investment requirements and had been set with the PSBR, not the needs of the businesses, firmly in mind. When they complained, they were told that such 'public sector constraints' were an inevitable consequence of their nationalized status and the only way to relax them would be to set the industries 'free in the market-place'. Making life unnecessarily unpleasant for the nationalized industries thus became a convenient spur to a change in management attitudes towards denationalization.

At the beginning of the programme, nationalized industries did not line up to be sold off. Equally, however, only BGC was determinedly and persistently obstructive (over its showrooms and the Wytch Farm oilfield). Had others followed this example, it is unlikely that so much would have been achieved in the Government's first term. It is now possible to detect in the later candidates a mixture of acquiescence and enthusiasm. This has not depended solely upon the power of ministerial patronage, as with Sir Philip Shelbourne at Britoil and Lord King at BA. Although such factors have played a part, most enterprises will be taken into the private sector by much the same management as ran them in the public sector. More significant, mainly because it seems to have penetrated far deeper down the managerial hierarchy than ministerial appointment runs, has been the apparent transformation of outlook about status. Suddenly, faced with an owner which can see nothing good in nationalized industries, the mood in certain industries seems to have swung decisively in favour of joining the private sector on the best possible terms. This changed outlook can be only partly explained in terms of management simply watching the way in which the political wind is blowing. Perhaps the most striking case has been BT, a relatively late candidate for sale after much discussion of liberalization, which has taken the initiative in explaining the gains from denationalization and in countering the trade unions' campaign of opposition.

Denationalization obviously becomes a much easier task for the Government if management can be converted. But such an advantage comes at the expense of exposing the inner tensions within the privatization programme, particularly about the relative priorities attached to denationalization and liberalization. Is the main objective to transfer the enterprise into the private sector, at the best possible price for the taxpayer? Or is it to secure improvements in industrial efficiency by stimulating competition, in which case the issues of *whether* the existing nationalized industry ought to be broken up, of what should happen to statutory restrictions on competition, and of the nature of any future regulatory arrangements, ought to be settled prior to sale? If such issues are not faced then, they may later prove much more difficult to resolve.

Initially, the emphasis appeared to be heavily upon the transfer of ownership and the immediate benefits to the PSBR. As the programme has grown, however, the Government has increasingly stressed the competition and efficiency issues. Similarly, there has developed an awareness amongst commentators that the two arms of privatization policy do not necessarily point in the same direction and can come into conflict. The classic case is BA, the denationalization statute for which was passed in 1980 but whose future shape is now open to doubt given the CAA's decision to recommend a reallocation of routes between British airlines prior to sale. But for the recession, BA would have been sold intact sometime in 1981: here is a clear case of the conflict between maximizing proceeds and using privatization as an instrument of competition policy because BA would be worth much more with its existing routes as well as its physical assets. In contrast, the case of BT has been resolved decisively in favour of ownership transfer.

Amidst the welter of polemics concerning 'privatization good' or 'privatization bad', two sets of issues have been neglected: first, the process of implementation and, second, the interaction between enterprise conduct and public policy in the post-privatization setting. It is the purpose of this book to address such issues, not least because they will increase in significance as the programme moves into the public enterprise 'heartlands'. There are three chapters on aspects of implementation which relate to the programme as a whole: David Heald on the 'public money' dimension; Craig Pickering on the mechanics of disposal; and David Thomas on the trade union response. Then, there are two case studies, one focusing on an industry in the midst of implementation (John Kay on the privatization of BT), and the other on industries at a much more speculative stage (Michael

Webb on the electricity supply and gas industries), which naturally straddle the boundary between implementation and post-privatization events. Finally, David Steel tackles the implications of hybridity (mixed public/private ownership) for future relationships between the Government and denationalized enterprises and questions whether the new ministerial resolve to sell the residual shareholdings disposes of the dilemmas which he identifies.

Other than a shared conviction that the issues considered here are highly important and deserve much greater study than they have received so far, this book has no common 'line'. Indeed, the individual authors would be unlikely to agree on many substantive points and they, not the Royal Institute of Public Administration, are responsible for the views expressed in their signed contributions. On behalf of all the contributors, the editors would like to thank the sponsoring bodies which funded the Research Workshop in April 1984 and those whose attendance made it such a stimulating and enjoyable occasion.

Given the rapid pace of developments, it should be noted that the chapters were revised immediately after the Workshop and that the final versions were agreed around the end of June 1984. Consequently, they do not refer, *inter alia*, to the Enterprise Oil flotation or to the information becoming available in July about the arrangements for the BT sale. But the salience of the book as a contribution to the debate can be grasped by noting David Steel's questions about the use of the government shareholdings and special shares, and Craig Pickering's scepticism about 'small shareholders'.

NOTES

1 See the lists of abbreviations on pages 9-10.

2

Privatization and Public Money

David Heald

Clarifying Concepts and Context

'Privatization' is an umbrella term for a diverse set of policies, albeit linked through an underlying judgement in favour of strengthening the 'market' at the expense of the 'state'. Yet it is a concept of crystal clarity when compared to that of 'public money'. To avoid this chapter becoming an exercise in taxonomy, many of the practical ambiguities will have to be sidestepped. What it aims to clarify are the various ways in which privatization measures impinge upon governmental finances, so that the parameters for subsequent empirical research can be established. It makes no attempt to provide comprehensive quantitative 'answers'. To the extent that these are feasible for past financial years, access to hitherto unpublished data would be essential. Prospectively, such estimates would be heavily contingent upon assumptions as to how the privatization programme will develop and to its practical consequences. More modestly, this chapter seeks to establish the types of linkages between privatization and public money which ought to be quantified in such an exercise.

Despite this book's focus solely upon the privatization of public enterprises, the present concern with public money necessitates brief reference to the four major components of privatization, namely, charging; contracting-out; denationalization and load-shedding; and liberalization (Heald 1983). In discussing public enterprises, the main emphasis will naturally be upon denationalization and liberalization. Yet there are important interconnections which mean that neither charging nor contracting-out can be ignored. For example, the elimination of subsidy through higher charges and/or cost reduction would be a pre-condition for transferring a heavily subsidized public enterprise such as BR into the private sector as a viable free-standing unit (as opposed to on a least-subsidy franchising basis). Contracting out of airport services via franchises whilst retaining public ownership of airport infrastructure received prominent attention in Foster's (1984) evaluation of the alternative methods by which the Government's intention to privatize the BAA might be effected. If these two policies were implemented, and they achieved their claimed benefits, there would be, other things being equal, less claim on public money for subsidy and higher profits, respectively.

In contrast, policies of denationalization and liberalization can readily be shown to have more ambiguous implications for public money than appears at first sight. Straightforwardly, denationalization generates proceeds for the Exchequer from asset sales and, where the public enterprise has taken the form of a public corporation, further reduces both the public expenditure planning total and the PSBR through the exclusion of its external finance (or in some cases its capital expenditure: see Steel and Heald 1984a). The longer term implications are, however, far more difficult to estimate. If, for example, denationalization were to lead to the more rapid contraction of a declining industry, there would be second-round effects in the form of additional public expenditure on redundancy payments, social security benefits, infrastructural adjustment and industrial promotion (Peacock and Shaw 1981). Such items will appear elsewhere in the accounts, in a diffused and difficult-to-connect form.

The impact of liberalization depends crucially upon the assumptions which are made about the post-privatization setting. If energetically implemented, such a policy would prevent the erstwhile public monopoly operator from pursuing policies of cross-subsidization in order to maintain unprofitable parts of its network (as, for example, in the case of buses). Either such services would be abandoned or some explicit subsidy arrangement involving direct claims upon public money would have to be devised. A major tension (Steel 1984) within the Government's privatization programme hinges around whether cross-subsidization is one of the inherent weaknesses of public ownership, to be purged through privatization, or whether it should be built, at least in part, into the new arrangements, as in the case of the emergency call and public call box conditions in BT's licence (DTI 1984).

Public money is an evocative phrase rather than a precise concept. Rhetoric about the respective merits of public and private inevitably obscures the complex interrelationship between the public and private sectors. Issues of ownership and control are often difficult to disentangle. It is difficult enough to specify what is owned or spent by the state: witness, for example, the way in which the agonized debate of the mid-1970s about the excessive levels of public expenditure in the UK relative to other countries owed much to misunderstandings about definitions and their coverage (Heald 1983; Imber and Todd 1983). Definitional problems aside, it would be completely wrong to treat the £126.4bn. planning total and the projected 42% public expenditure/GDP ratio for 1984-85 (Treasury 1984a) as reliable indexes of 'state activity'. Crucially, they pick up only those public policy interventions which take the form of public expenditure.

In a climate in which holding down public expenditure totals becomes a political imperative, it is ever more necessary to monitor the policy substitutes for public expenditure. Although confiscation is of marginal relevance, tax expenditures and coerced private expenditures are central to prospective developments. Through policies of widespread privatization, especially in the social sphere, a committed and energetic government could significantly reduce the public expenditure/GDP ratio. However, many of the proposals (such as those of the CPRS on the welfare state [*The Economist* 1982]) envisage that the withdrawal of public provision would be accompanied by the introduction of tax expenditures (e.g. tax relief on private health insurance subscriptions) and coerced private expenditures (e.g. compulsory insurance). There is an obvious temptation for governments to proclaim control of explicit public expenditure but to allow unchecked growth of items which are neither planned nor properly counted.

Budgetary stress played a significant role in building up the momentum of the Government's programme for privatizing public enterprises: the proceeds of special asset sales were seen as a welcome bonus which, because of the way the figures are presented, had the equivalent effect to a cut in public expenditure. Contortions with PSBR/EFL rules reflected either genuine misunderstanding of the issues by ministers[1] or a convenient blindness, which allowed privatization to be promoted on pragmatic grounds which might be made to appeal to the nationalized industries themselves.[2] With the Government now shifting the tenor of its advocacy of privatization towards the promotion of competition and greater efficiency, it is an appropriate time to look back on the links between privatization and public money. It would be wrong to argue that the Government's sole concern[3] has been to sell the family silver (to use Mr John Moore's [1983] phrase) but even more mistaken to deny that the effects on public expenditure totals and the PSBR have not been a significant consideration.

The Significance of the PSBR Rules

Any system of accounting must by its very nature draw lines, meaning that individual items are classified on one side or the other. A fundamental test of good design is that classification rules do not of themselves distort economic and financial decisions. Governmental budgeting systems are dominated by the annuality rule: that the unit of time is the financial year. However inevitable such a rule can be argued to be, an unfortunate consequence of its application is that disproportionate significance becomes attached to the exact timing of transactions. Even in the case of budget-financed organizations, this problem has received widespread publicity, particularly about local authority capital expenditure. With each local authority facing a cash limit ceiling, such a system of control has a bias towards aggregate underspending. Moreover, the uncertainties attached to the phasing of capital works mean that potential underspendings are often 'rectified' by the advancing of flexible but low priority schemes. Central government's attempts to control the aggregate can be disruptive of local programmes, priorities and efficiency. Yet even modest concessions on carry-over provisions can make it much more difficult to 'hit' the central total.

For trading organizations within the public sector, the clash between the annuality rule and the time horizon relevant to the efficient operation of the business is more dramatic: the analogy of trying to land a jumbo on a postage stamp has been suggested. Not least, the public corporations represent some of the most capital intensive sectors of the entire economy, often being characterized by long project lead times and asset lives. The nature of the interface between the finances of such public enterprises and those of the Exchequer is therefore crucial. Yet its design shows little evidence of forethought and attracted little public attention until its damaging consequences became evident (and, by then, unlikely to be tackled for they have provided a convenient spur to privatization).

The PSBR rules have diverted attention from the crucial task of sustaining a viable control framework for the public enterprise sector. The emphasis now attached to EFLs, both individually and in aggregate, is entirely inappropriate in the context of trading as opposed to budget-financed organizations. Whatever views are taken about the merits of the 1978 White Paper on nationalized industries (Treasury 1978), there can be little doubt that the subsequent preoccupation with the PSBR and hence EFLs undermined the process of implementation. The 'rules of the game' have become increasingly dominated by short-term considerations, as reflected in EFLs, and by the ever-expanding list of candidates for privatization. Investment rules such as the RRR, pricing policies such as LRMC pricing and even financial targets (except in support of EFLs) have been effectively downgraded. Though never withdrawn, the 1978 White Paper has been superseded by events, with its 'public appearances' now reserved mainly for occasions when it can be cited in support of particular positions. A new White Paper has been urgently required for some time but will not be produced because such an exercise would be regarded as diverting energies and attention away from the commitment to privatization.

Following the 1977 narrowing of the public expenditure definition, which took out the capital expenditure of the nationalized industries, it has been their external finance which has 'counted'. Government subsidies, loans and capital subscriptions, market and overseas borrowing, and the capital value of newly leased assets are now included in the 'planning total'.[4] Despite its familiarity in both official publications and political debate, the term 'nationalized industries' is in fact very imprecise. Which organizations are classified as nationalized industries for public expenditure purposes is a matter decided by the Treasury, and is subject to change from time to time. Nationalized industries are a sub-set of a wider group of public corporations, an organizational form adopted in the UK for diverse purposes. Other public corporations have been grouped together into three lists (I, II and III),[5] reflecting different degrees of integration into Exchequer finances

(Steel and Heald 1984a). (List I treatment is identical to that of the nationalized industries, as described above.) An important recent change has been the reclassification of the regional water authorities in England and Wales as nationalized industries, having previously been in List III.[6] Consequently, their capital expenditure has been removed from the public expenditure totals, with government loans and capital subscription (if there were any) being included instead.

Judgements about classification are inevitable, with the consequence that discussion about the resulting totals ought to be conducted with due recognition of the fact that some lines will be arbitrary. That kind of sophistication has been sorely lacking in the debate about the impact of EFLs on nationalized industries, with the PSBR rules seemingly treated as inviolable, rather than judgemental.[7] In particular, many of the difficulties have stemmed from the UK's tradition of taking a broad view of the 'public sector', whereas the international focus has been on 'general government'. There is a close parallel between the misunderstandings about public expenditure definitions in the mid-1970s and the 1979-81 controversy about the impact of the PSBR rules on nationalized industries' capital programmes. The problem arose almost accidentally, being rooted in part in the reliance in the UK on the public corporation model. Even when the state has owned 100% of the equity of Companies Act companies, such as RR and BNFL, they have not been consolidated into public sector accounts and have been treated by the CSO as part of the private sector.[8] The only items affecting public expenditure totals would be transactions between such enterprises and the Exchequer, namely subsidies, loans and capital subscription, but not their capital programmes nor their non-Exchequer external finance.

The official explanation for this different treatment, that the public ownership of BL and RR was intended only to be temporary, should be taken with a large pinch of salt.[9] Whilst the debate on the nationalized industries' external financing was at its height, RR did in fact raise private finance outside the PSBR. Moreover, if the earlier dichotomy between public corporation/Companies Act company had been consistently applied when the privatization programme took shape, an organization should have been promptly excluded from the PSBR once its legal form changed. However, this practice was not adopted, neither when the National Freight Corporation became the National Freight Company nor when BA became a plc. The new rule has been only to exclude when control passes to the private sector, a condition taken to be fulfilled when a majority of shares has been sold.[10] The 'benefits to the PSBR' have thus been presented as linked intrinsically to denationalization.

Far less attention has been paid to the viability of the overall control framework for nationalized industries. This should be directed towards securing efficiency, broadly defined so as to recognize that monopoly, externality and distributional issues mean that profitability alone is not a reliable test. If such a system were working satisfactorily, the financial flows between the Exchequer and each enterprise would depend upon the latter's results and prospects. In particular, its self-financing ratio and external financing requirement would depend upon the size of its internally-generated funds relative to those capital requirements which could be justified on the basis of prospective DCF returns. In other words, EFLs would be determined by other parts of the control system, rather than being the dominant factor. However, lack of faith in the rest of the system of control has encouraged (sometimes cavalier) reliance upon EFLs. If severe doubts are entertained about the profitability of capital programmes, there will naturally be far less concern should EFLs induce cutbacks. Indeed, the overriding concern about totals has led to a surprising lack of probing of the inefficient business practices and creative accounting adopted as methods of living with such constraints.

Since the election of the Conservative Government in 1979, the aggregate EFL has often been projected to 'disappear' in the last year of the Survey, only for the next White Paper to roll that horizon forward one year. Table 1 shows the projected turnaround in nationalized industries' external finance planned by successive White Papers.[11] 'External finance' has been treated as a public expenditure programme, but one which is highly undesirable and should be eliminated as quickly as possible. The approach to setting EFLs has thus been top-down, emphasizing totals rather than composition. This disregards the diverse nature of both items and organizations included therein: from subsidy to finance for profitable investment, and from the NCB to BT. It is an indefensible position to argue that the nationalized sector should be entirely self-financing each year on trading and capital accounts combined, certainly without basing that claim upon a careful analysis of the individual enterprises concerned. Not least, the denationalization programme is now proceeding with sufficient pace for changes in the composition of the sector not to be acknowledged in such discussions. Whatever the case might be for greater profitability and more negative EFLs for the electricity supply industry, cancelling out the positive EFLs of BR and the NCB should not be part of it.

Terminology is potentially misleading: profitability is not the same as 100% self-financing, most of all at the aggregate level. 'Self-sufficiency' (Likierman 1984) is also confusing, not least because it sounds a desirable condition. Although the policy of reducing aggregate EFLs to zero has not succeeded, it has achieved a significant turnaround: for example, the 'Government, market and overseas borrowing (net)' of the nationalized industries fell by 75% in cost terms from 1978-79 to 1983-84 (Treasury 1984b, 7).[12] In contrast, assistance to the coal industry has risen markedly, providing a reminder of the extent to which the EFLs for the NCB and BR now dominate totals (£2039m. compared to an aggregate of £1881m. in 1984-85).

Moreover, certain ironies can be detected in current developments. First,

TABLE 1 The projected turnaround in nationalized industries' external finance

	Financial Year (£m.)											
	1975-6	1976-7	1977-8	1978-9	1979-80	1980-1	1981-2	1982-3	1983-4	1984-5	1985-6	1986-7
1979 White Paper (1978 survey prices)				1,000	800	600	500	850				
1980 White Paper (1979 survey prices)					2,300	1,450	700	200	(400)			
1981 White Paper (1980 survey prices)	4,756	3,275	1,822	2,367	2,613	2,500	1,750	750	50			
1982 White Paper (cash)		2,243	1,416	2,020	2,613	2,900	3,393	2,739	2,570	2,100		
1983 White Paper (cash)			1,448	2,059	2,649	2,877	3,254	2,253	2,625	2,261	1,803	
1984 White Paper (cash)				2,349	2,999	3,221	3,553	2,143	2,500	1,881	1,145	91

Note: The entries are difficult to compare from one White Paper to the next, initially because of the moving price base and then because of the switch to cash planning.

Source: Treasury 1979a, 1980, 1981, 1982a, 1983, 1984a.

the sale of profitable enterprises will increase the aggregate EFL, for the 'contribution' of, for example, Britoil and BT will be lost in later years. Second, the profitable enterprises have been forced through EFLs to achieve levels of self-financing far higher than they would have chosen independently. The Government's rationale has been to curb the PSBR, partly because of the assumed link with money supply growth and partly as a method of avoiding further pressure on the private sector through higher interest rates. After denationalization, even on the hybrid model, it seems unlikely that these enterprises would consider such high levels of self-financing appropriate. Resort to the capital market for part of their investment requirements would thus lead to a higher combined public and private borrowing requirement, with implications for both the money supply and interest rates. Third, a familiar (but not the only) argument for not allowing the nationalized industries direct access to the capital market has been that this would in some sense crowd out the private sector. However, the Government's enthusiasm for disposing of public sector assets of various forms must be diverting funds from other uses.

Asset Sales and Public Expenditure Totals

The Medium-Term Financial Strategy, with its targets for the PSBR in future years, provides a framework within which PESC decisions must now be taken. More public attention than ever before is directed at the planning total, with the movement of this cash figure being interpreted as a test of the Government's resolve to hold down the real level of public spending.

Asset sales are a method of reducing the planning total, having the same effect as equivalent reductions in current expenditure. At this level, no distinctions are made between current and capital, so that the accounting system treats them as substitutes. The 'special sales of assets' programme thus performs a dual function: it provides tangible evidence that the Government is fulfilling its promise to roll back the state; and it makes any given planning total easier to achieve. The decision in the Conservative Government's first (one year) White Paper (Treasury 1979b) to set targets reflected both these factors. However, such a method of holding down the planning total was not in itself new: the previous Labour Government had sold part of the public shareholding in BP in 1977-78 for precisely the same reason. Throughout the Conservative Government's first term, the proceeds were in reality fairly insignificant, especially when the items so classified are closely inspected.

The prospects for the second term are markedly different, as evidenced by the publicity attached to the £10bn. disposal target which was announced well ahead of the publication of the 1984 White Paper (Treasury 1984a). The 1984-85 planning total was contained in the 1984 White Paper at £126.4bn., the figure inherited from the 1983 White Paper (Treasury 1983). An increase in the target for special sales of assets from £1,500m. to

£1,900m. was a contributory factor. Earlier, the July 1983 package had increased the 1983-84 target by £500m., leading to the sale of further tranches of shares in BP and C&W. Even so, it is necessary to place the annual target of £2bn. a year during this Parliament in the context of a planning total of c.£130bn. However, given its sensitivity to charges of pillaging the family silver, it is perhaps not surprising that the Government's concerted effort to redefine the terms of the privatization debate, towards competition and efficiency and away from the PSBR, coincided with the launching of a larger and more systematic programme of asset sales.

Examination of the items credited to this programme draws attention to a number of important issues. Table 2 provides a structured analysis of the total proceeds for the years 1979-80 to 1983-84. Three categories are distinguished: proceeds from the sale of shares in erstwhile nationalized industries and of public shareholdings; other asset sales; and revenue offsets. In the first four financial years, the first category generated only £1,147m. The apparent excellent targeting in 1979-80 is revealed to have been due to the inclusion of advance sales of BNOC's oil, a manoeuvre which unwound itself in 1981-82, throwing the entire programme 'negative'. Some of the other items are also dubious, having little to do with the privatization programme (e.g. receipts from oil licensing rounds). The new 'line', having been created, attracted items which might have taken place anyway and been classified elsewhere. In that sense, it is a 'gross' figure, not measuring net impact on the planning total.

One of the difficulties of interpretation relates to the word 'special' in 'special asset sales'. In their ordinary business, public sector organizations buy and sell assets, almost on a daily basis. Two issues thus arise: how can 'special' be distinguished from routine;[13] and where in the accounting system will disposal transactions be recorded? It might have been ruled that only those items clearly linked to privatization initiatives would have been classified as special, though Table 2 indicates that this practice was not adopted. By far the largest such initiative is not so classified, namely the sale of council housing (now running at around £1.5bn. a year) which is treated as an offset to the housing programmes. Most important, however, is the fact that items are only classified as 'special' should the proceeds accrue directly to the Exchequer. Consequently, a wide range of asset disposals is missed, especially in the public enterprise field, even when they represent the implementation of Government instructions. The amounts involved thus 'disappear' into the organizations, with the Exchequer only receiving the benefit to the extent that such disposals result in lower EFLs (i.e. less positive or more negative). To the extent that such clawback has taken place, detailed examination of the various disposals of, for example, BR, BSC and BL[14] must therefore be undertaken. In some important cases, however, such as BGC's offshore oil assets, this problem has been tackled directly by compulsorily transferring them without compensation to a government department, prior to disposal.

TABLE 2 Proceeds from special sales of assets (£m. cash)

	1979-80	1980-1	1981-2	1982-3	1983-4[6]
TARGET [1]	1000	500	500	600	750
ACTUAL					
1 PRIVATIZED NATIONALIZED INDUSTRIES[2] AND PUBLIC SHAREHOLDINGS	336	126	305	380	1099
Sale of shares in British Petroleum	276		8[3]		543
" " " held by National Enterprise Board	37	83	2		
" " " in British Aerospace		43			
" " " in Cable & Wireless			182		263
" " " in British Sugar Corporation			44		
" " " in Amersham International			64		
" " " in National Freight Company			5		
" " " in Britoil				334[4]	293
" " " in Associated British Ports				46	
" " " in other companies	23				

2 OTHER ASSET SALES	34	279	189	108	58
Sale of land and buildings owned by various public bodies[5]	34	56	88	31	27
Sale of motorway service area leases		28	19	4	1
Receipts from 7th and 8th rounds of offshore oil licensing		195		33	19
Sale of oil stockpile			63	33	
Sale of other stocks			19	7	11
TOTAL 1 + 2	**370**	**405**	**494**	**488**	**1157**
3 REVENUE OFFSETS					
Advance payments to BNOC for oil	622	(49)	(573)		
Stamp Duty and VAT	7				
GRAND TOTAL (1 + 2 + 3)	**999**	**356**	**(79)**	**488**	**1157**

Notes:

1 Comparison of actual proceeds against target is complicated by the switch from volume to cash planning in the 1982 public expenditure White Paper (Treasury 1982a). The target figures listed in the table ignore this complication, as have Government pronouncements. They are taken from the Treasury's *Economic Progress Report* (Treasury 1982b) and do not in all cases agree with the figures in successive public expenditure White Papers. The 1983-84 target, taken from (Treasury 1984), was increased to £1250m. in July 1983.

2 To these totals, there need to be added the proceeds of various sales which have remained within the businesses concerned, for instance BR and BSC, even if effectively offset by equivalent reductions in Exchequer finance.

3 The Government's nil-paid rights in the 1981 rights issue.

4 Includes repayment of a debenture of £88m. with interest.

5 New towns, water authorities, Property Services Agency, Crown Agents, Forestry Commission, Land Settlement Association.

6 Provisional outturns.

Source: Treasury 1982b, 1983, 1984a: provisional outturns for 1983-84 were supplied by the Treasury.

Perhaps the fundamental problem is that public sector financial reporting suffers from a lack of clarity about what is measured and why. It lacks the secure base provided by capital maintenance concepts for private sector accounting. This point is illustrated by the definitional, presentational and theoretical problems surrounding the measurement and interpretation of the PSBR. There is the question of its coverage, particularly in relation to the external financing of public enterprises. The troublesome question of netting practices also looms large. The usual example relates to whether charges are deducted from gross expenditure or treated as a source of revenue. The disposal of public sector assets has highlighted the parallel issue of whether such proceeds are netted against the planning total, or treated as a source of financing. With asset sales of £2bn. a year, a PSBR reported as £7bn. on the 'netting' practice would appear as £9bn. on the 'financing' practice. The Treasury and Civil Service Committee (1984) has sharply criticized the netting practice as thoroughly misleading. But strange rules can produce strange defences, especially if you are a closet Keynesian:

> The sale of public corporation shares and council houses has allowed the government to do good by stealth, by running a bigger psbr than the published figure. There is thus merit in continuing the present curious rule that asset sales reduce the psbr rather than financing it, given the constraints of the government's Medium-Term Financial Strategy (Johnson 1983, 3).

If such a view is to be accepted, it says little for the integrity or self-conviction of either the Government or its critics.

Quite apart from such problems of presentation, there is the important theoretical question of 'which PSBR' is judged to be relevant to the conduct of monetary policy. Leaving aside the Keynesian constructs of the constant-employment and demand-weighted PSBRs, the nominal PSBR (the figure always cited in the Medium-Term Financial Strategy) can be supplemented by the constant-price PSBR and the inflation-adjusted PSBR. The first of these simply removes the effect of inflation by expressing each year at a common price basis, whilst the second sets off against the nominal PSBR the gains to the public sector from the effects of inflation on its nominal debt.[15] Friedman (1980, 56-57) is on record as arguing that it is the inflation-adjusted PSBR, not the nominal PSBR, which exerts the major effect on interest rates for any given monetary growth. For much of the 1970s, the inflation-adjusted PSBR was a negative figure, dramatically transforming the high nominal PSBR and making the public sector a net saver.

Depending on which measure of the PSBR is used, entirely different assessments of fiscal stance can be reached. Developing this argument, Hills (1984) has constructed an (admittedly rough and ready) balance sheet for the UK public sector as a whole. His calculations for the changes in the real net worth of the public sector are dramatically different from those provided by the nominal PSBR: reductions of £7bn. in 1981-82 and £26bn. in 1982-83, much greater than the nominal PSBRs of roughly £9bn. in each year. In contrast, the previous six years showed increases in the public sector's net worth despite the high nominal PSBRs which were then generating so much concern. The dramatic turnaround owes much to lower levels of public investment, the rapid depletion of the asset of North Sea oil, the growth of unfunded pension liabilities and a lower inflation-induced reduction in the real value of the public sector's nominal debt.

What the vigorous programme of asset sales has done has been to draw increased attention to conceptual and practical weaknesses in public sector accounting. However advisable such disposals might be held to be on other grounds of public policy, the accounting system ought to be recording the changes in the public sector's financial position in a much more sophisticated and sensitive way. Failure to do this can have damaging consequences in terms both of obfuscating the macroeconomic debate and of generating incentives for particular transactions which have little to do with the search for greater efficiency.

What Are Public Assets Really Worth?

Political controversy about the denationalization programme tends to be conducted on two levels: the issue of principle as to whether assets should be sold; and the question of whether a 'fair value' has been obtained. Opponents of the programme have suggested that the Government has been selling public sector assets at knock-down prices, undertaking such an asset-stripping operation in order to generate cash for cuts in taxation and providing generous commissions for its City friends. In response to this charge, the Government is insistent that such assets will be more efficiently managed in the private sector, with benefits for the economy as a whole. Given the size of the denationalization programme, valuation of the assets involved is extremely difficult. However, some commentators would argue that the only valid valuation of any asset or enterprise is the price which the market is willing to pay. Consequently, the only meaning of 'fair' is held to be the market valuation. Provided, therefore, that the offers for sale are properly structured, there can be no question of the Exchequer receiving less than the assets are worth. Capital issues can, of course, be mismanaged, leading to heavy over-subscription at a fixed price but such problems of judging the market are familiar from the private sector's own experience.

However, there are important reasons for being sceptical about this line of argument. The programme is so large and comprehensive that, in terms of size alone, it involves exploring relatively uncharted territory. 'Privatization equity', on present plans, is likely to constitute a significant proportion of the total net new issues of UK ordinary shares for the rest of the decade. There are unresolved questions about the extent to which they will 'crowd out' private sector equity issues and how portfolios will be readjusted when the Treasury cuts back on new gilts.

Being privatization equity, such issues will enjoy a high public and political profile. Because they have been under full public ownership and some of them occupy strategic positions in the economy, the performance and behaviour of (at least the most important) successor enterprises will be observed closely. The political controversy surrounding their status might be expected to exert downward pressure on the valuation of these enterprises. Nevertheless, one of the surprising features of the programme during the Government's first term was the lack of seriousness apparently attached by would-be investors to the Labour Party's threats of renationalization, either with no compensation or 'with compensation of no more than that received when the assets were sold'.[16] Even before the Party's internal feuds made it extremely unlikely that it would win the election due in 1984, this possibility seems to have been heavily discounted. One of the Government's significant achievements was thus to break through a difficult psychological barrier, building up confidence in the financial community that its programme was irreversible.

However, there are issues at stake more subtle than threats of renationalization. Only experience will tell whether the Government's self-denying ordinance not to intervene in the commercial affairs of hybrid enterprises in which it is the massively dominant shareholder will stand the test of events and political change. Even if disposal of these 'residual shareholdings' is effected, the fortunes of the most significant enterprises will be heavily conditioned by governmental decisions, especially on contracts and on regulation. Having examined the conditions for effective regulation of BT, the Littlechild Report concluded:

> The main purpose of regulation is to protect domestic and small business subscribers against BT's dominant market position. Improving efficiency is a means to that end. Prevention of excessive profits to shareholders is *not* a relevant consideration, since expected profits will be reflected in the price of BT's shares at flotation, so shareholders will not earn an excessive return on their investment (Littlechild 1983, 1).

In practice, however, the plans for BT's flotation are progressing amidst major uncertainty about the future regulatory climate. There is an obvious trade-off for the Government between maximizing the proceeds from disposal (by preserving monopoly power virtually intact) and subordinating them to other policy objectives (by vigorously pursuing liberalization along the lines advocated by the Beesley and Littlechild Reports [Beesley 1981; Littlechild 1983]).

Even if 'fair value' would be obtained for BT's shares under conditions of regulatory certainty, the proceeds are likely to be depressed when so many issues remain outstanding. Whether 'regulation with a light rein' will be the outcome of current developments may depend in part on public perceptions about whether the sale price was appropriate. A future government, hostile to privatization, might opt for tougher regulation rather than renationalization. Alternatively, policies of more vigorous liberalization might be advocated with a motive of penalizing the private shareholders.

Suspicion that the taxpayer's interest has been compromised is likely to be fuelled by changes in accounting policies immediately prior to sale. BT's changes in the financial year 1983-84 (mainly shortening asset lives and ceasing to capitalize certain items) involve a departure from accounting standards (BT 1984).[17] Although such changes *may* be justified by the transformation of competitive environment, public awareness of the amount of discretion involved in corporate reporting has already been awakened by the transition to inflation accounting.[18]

Attention is likely to focus upon the relationship between disposal price, subsequent market valuation and the replacement cost of assets shown by the published accounts. It is understood that Britoil has internally valued its assets on a DCF basis at twice the valuation underlying the under-subscribed sale by tender. More publicly, figures have been cited by BGC for the value of its share in Wytch Farm which were of the order of three times the actual sale price.[19] Even allowing for the possibly self-interested nature of such figures, questions are likely to be asked by the PAC about these discrepancies. In particular, setting sales targets by financial year and attempting to force through such sales, irrespective of market conditions, can be argued to impose a considerable cost in terms of proceeds foregone. If a company is located in a sector with high systematic risk,[20] its share price will demonstrate greater volatility than the market portfolio as a whole. In terms

FIGURE 1 Market capitalizations of denationalized enterprises.

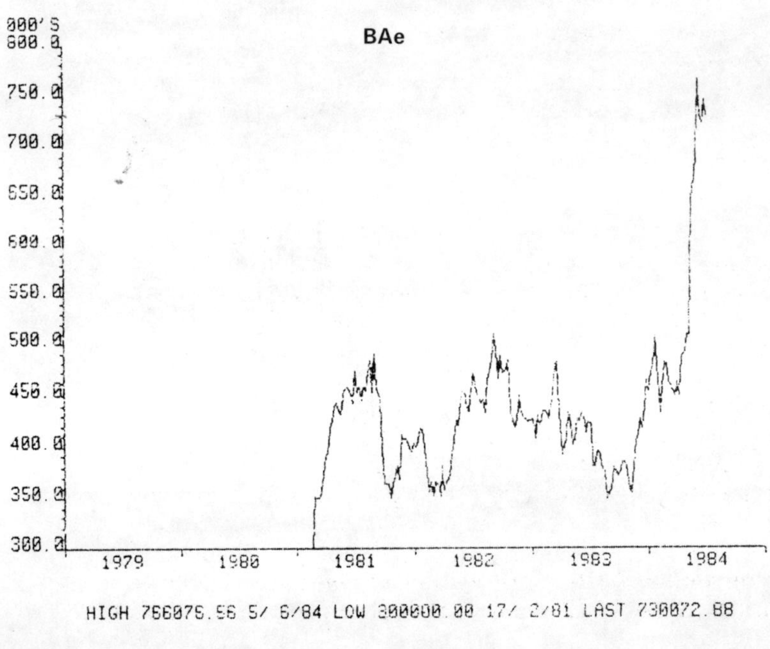

FIGURE 1 continued

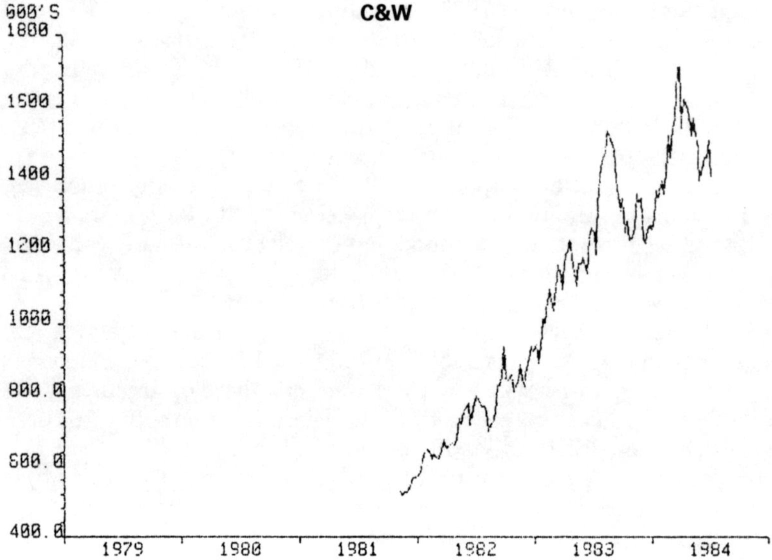

HIGH 1769999.00 20/ 3/84 LOW 518399.75 17/11/81 LAST 1408499.00

HIGH 151999.94 21/ 6/83 LOW 95499.94 9/ 3/82 LAST 120499.94

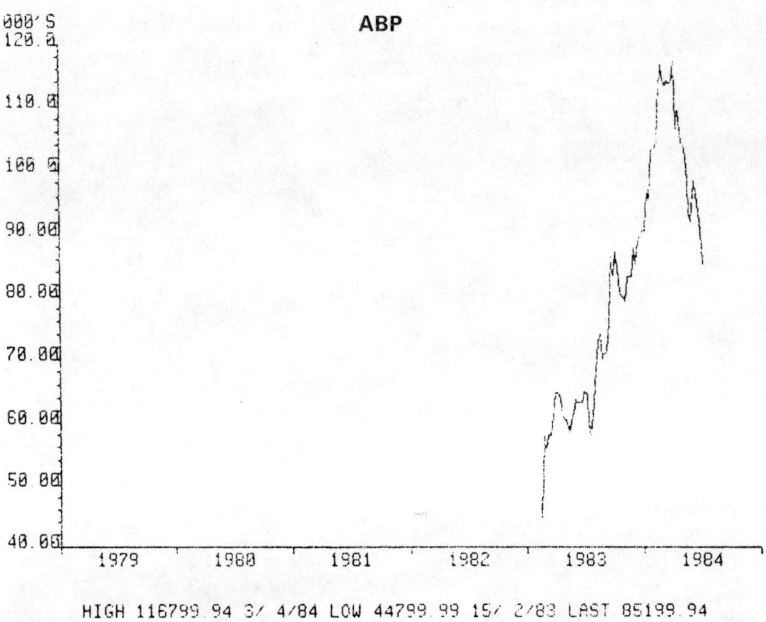

Source: Thanks are due to Datastream International Ltd, and in particular to Stephen Phillips, for providing these graphs.

of maximizing proceeds to the Exchequer for any given regulatory policy, the timing of disposals becomes a factor of significance.

Sufficient time has now elapsed since the early sales for there to be historical evidence available on how the capital market has valued the denationalized enterprises. Figure 1 contains five graphs, one each for BAe, C&W, AI, Britoil and ABP. These show the market capitalizations of the companies, from the date of flotation to the 3 July 1984. Although the horizontal (time) axes have the same scale, the vertical (value) axes are very different, reflecting the variations in the size of the enterprises. Taking BAe as an example, the company was valued at £300m. on flotation but later peaked (in terms of the period shown) at £766m. on 5 June 1984 because of takeover proposals. Despite all the controversy about AI, it is C&W and ABP whose increasing capitalization raises the most serious doubts about whether the taxpayer received value for money. AI's honeymoon is now over and Britoil has see-sawed. Figure 2's graphs interpret movements in the denationalized companies' share prices relative to changes in the market as a whole, measured here by the *Financial Times* All-share Index. The differences in vertical scales should again be noted. The plotted line converts the ratio between the share price on the date of flotation and the Index to 100 and traces out subsequent relative movements. Thus, a value greater than 100 means that the share has out-performed the market, whilst less than 100

FIGURE 2 Share price relative to Financial Times all-share index (Own flotation date value = 100)

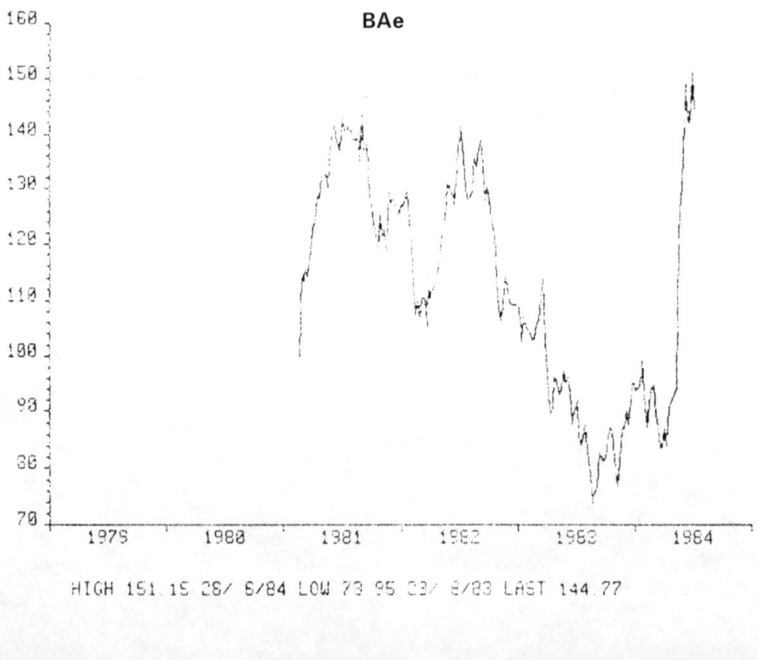

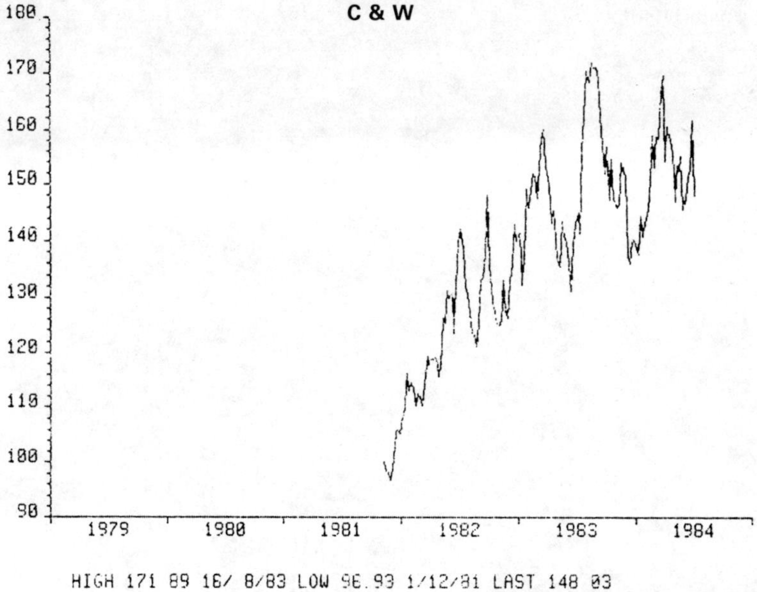
C & W
180
170
160
150
140
130
120
110
100
90
1979
1980
1981
1982
1983
1984
HIGH 171 89 16/ 8/83 LOW 96.93 1/12/81 LAST 148 03

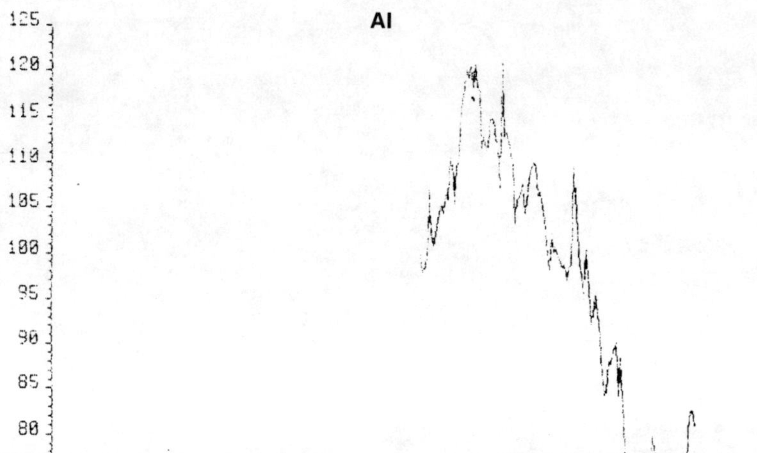
AI
125
120
115
110
105
100
95
90
85
80
75
70
1979
1980
1981
1982
1983
1984
HIGH 121 17 9/11/82 LOW 71 31 5/ 6/84 LAST 81 11

FIGURE 2 continued

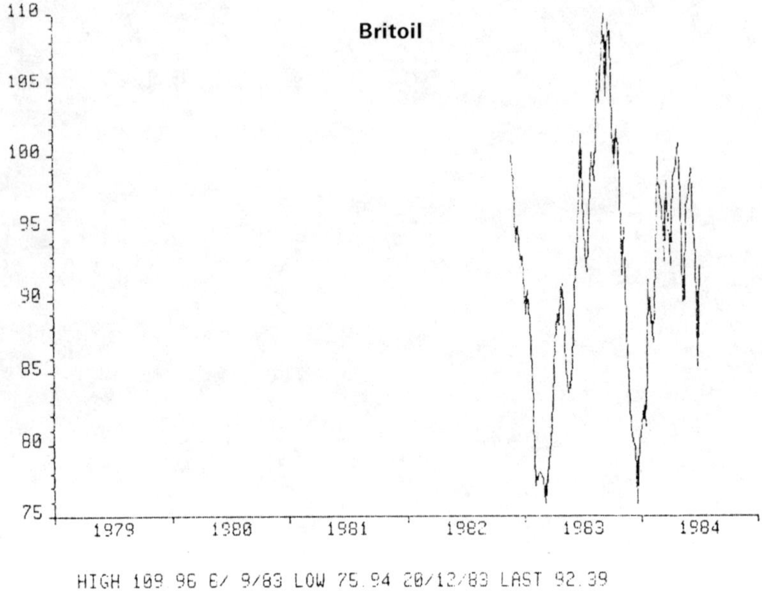

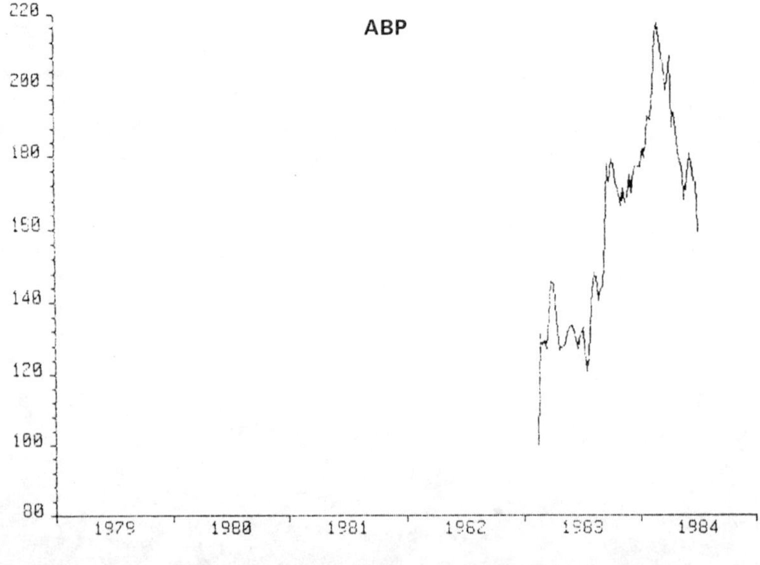

Source: Thanks are due to Datastream International Ltd, and in particular to Stephen Phillips, for providing these graphs.

means the converse. Again, C&W and ABP stand out alone (despite the second tranches of sales of the government shareholding) whilst BAe's record was less than convincing until it became the object of rival takeover plans. These Figures do not instil confidence that the market can readily value denationalized assets so that the taxpayer automatically receives what they are 'really worth'.

Another perspective upon the denationalized enterprises can be constructed by calculating the amounts of public money which have been invested in them. Subsequently, this can be compared with the proceeds of disposal, a step which will prompt questions about both past performance and the implementation of denationalization. The only published example to date is the PAC's analysis of BAe whose nationalization and partial denationalization were compressed into a short time period.[21] The task is obviously more laborious and problematical when enterprises have been in public ownership for long periods, especially if earlier bouts of restructuring have blurred financial relationships (for example, by assets being transferred between public sector bodies without financial compensation).

There is an obvious parallel with Henderson's painstaking work (1977) on the AGR and Concorde programmes, though the focus here would be on entire enterprises. Nevertheless, the methodological problems should not be underestimated, for example, what discount rates should be used to bring cash flows to a common date; how to treat 'privileges' such as the old BNOC's special position on North Sea licences and exemption from Petroleum Revenue Tax; and how to value the contribution of the enterprise to other public policy objectives (such as regional development, income distribution, support for domestic suppliers, employment maintenance and macroeconomic stability). In strictly financial (i.e. not cost benefit) terms, it seems likely that some of the results would look very bleak, a prediction prompted not least by the way in which underfunded pension liabilities have been wiping out much of the proceeds from some of the sales.[22]

When public policy decisions lead to drastic changes in organizational structure and environment, there will inevitably be certain costs of adjustment. Valuation of the full range of these costs is highly problematical. Fees and commissions paid to consultants and merchant banks are straightforward enough but measuring the opportunity costs of departmental and parliamentary time raises formidable difficulties. Even worse, there is no agreement, rather revolving fashions, about whether shocks to organizations imposed by restructuring exercises are inherently beneficial or dislocating.

Conclusion

Privatization thus has manifold direct and indirect links with public money. Without attempting to summarize the detailed argument, three concluding points will be made. First, with the programme gathering momentum, the tensions between liberalization and denationalization (especially as a money-raising exercise) have begun to receive more attention. Less noticed has been the danger that privatization will extend the use of policy substitutes for public expenditure, bringing private organizations even closer into this net. Second, there is a major research (and policy) task delineating carefully the cost and benefits of such policy changes. The laundering of figures prior to denationalization and superficial comparisons afterwards are to be expected but ought to be challenged. Third, and most importantly, the contribution which artificial and distortionary rules have played in promoting support for the denationalization of public enterprises ought to be noted by policy-makers and managers elsewhere in the public sector.

NOTES

1 For example, Mr Adam Butler (1979), then a Minister of State at the Department of Industry, described the external finance of the ESI as 'a drag on the nation's resources'.

2 See, for example, the emphasis placed on the PSBR argument for denationalization in Mr Patrick Jenkin's statement on the future of BT, reproduced in Department of Industry (1982).

3 Four major arguments can be detected in the Government's case for privatizing public enterprises: it will enhance economic freedom; it will increase efficiency; it will ease the problem of public sector pay; and it will reduce the PSBR. For an evaluation of these arguments, see Heald and Steel (1982).

4 It should be noted that there have been significant detailed changes since 1977. Steel and Heald (1984a) explain the conventions as at the 1984 White Paper (Treasury 1984a) and Imber and Todd (1983) show the changes between successive White Papers.

5 For the composition of these lists, see Treasury (1984a, Vol. II, 170). However, legal status is not paramount: List I also includes government trading funds (such as the ROFs and the Royal Mint) which are treated as public corporations for statistical and planning purposes.

6 The classification of the regional water authorities changed in both the 1983 and 1984 White Papers (Treasury 1983; 1984a): from List III to List I; and then from List I to nationalized industry status (using Steel and Heald's [1984a] terminology, from List IB to IA). There is no difference between the public expenditure treatment of Lists IA and IB.

7 However, it should be noted that some of the Treasury's worries, notably about implicit guarantees attaching to finance from private sources, had solid foundation.

8 C&W was the exception to this rule, being treated as a public corporation despite its limited company status (Treasury 1981).

9 Even if this explanation were accepted, the cases of the Radiochemical Centre Ltd. (now AI) and BNFL remain to be accounted for.

10 Steel (1984) raises a series of interesting questions about who controls the new hybrid enterprises, especially when the public shareholding remains just under 50%.

11 After the 1982 and 1983 White Papers moderated the projected turnarounds, it is interesting to note that the post-election 1984 White Paper has reverted to the earlier pattern (See Table 1). The old programme 5 (Government lending to the nationalized industries) has been abolished, with the external finance of nationalized industries being taken to the functional programme of their sponsoring department. The programme had already fallen into disuse, in favour of the more comprehensive table in Part 3 of each White Paper's Volume II (Treasury 1982a, 1983, 1984a).

12 It should be noted that the Treasury has started to describe the cost terms series (cash figures adjusted by the GDP deflator) as 'real terms'.

13 There is an obvious parallel with the accounting standards debate on the distinction between 'exceptional' and 'extraordinary' items.

14 Because of BL's incorporation as a Companies Act company, the chain through which the Exchequer benefits is different but parallel.

15 Calculations of the inflation-adjusted PSBR have been pioneered by the Bank of England, starting with Taylor and Threadgold (1979).

16 The phrase quoted here comes from the Labour Party's 1983 election manifesto (Labour Party 1983). Confusion about its intentions on renationalization was just one reflection of the bitter conflict between the Parliamentary Labour Party and the Annual Conference, and within the PLP itself.

17 There has already been extensive comment about the extent to which the preparation of BA's accounts for 1981-82 was influenced by a desire to concentrate adverse items in that year, so as to improve the pre-privatization results.

18 For an examination of claims that nationalized industries' accounts have been manipulated, see Likierman (1983).

19 See Michael Webb's discussion in Chapter 6.

20 The Capital Asset Pricing Model, now the conventional wisdom of business finance theory, suggests that total risk can be subdivided into unsystematic risk (specific to the security and which can be eliminated by a well-diversified portfolio) and systematic risk (which cannot be diversified away and is measured by the security's β, indicating whether it is more or less volatile than the market as a whole).

21 The PAC concluded that there had been an undiscounted loss to the Exchequer from the complete cycle of £80m. (PAC1982).

22 The Government's efforts to disperse share ownership (partly out of principle and partly as a tactical defence against threats of renationalization) have sacrificed some of the potential proceeds, by influencing the choice of methods of sale. These foregone revenues should be regarded as tax expenditures and valued (especially in the light of the predictable subsequent falls in the number of shareholders). Similarly, restrictions on the level of foreign ownership can be expected to depress sale proceeds.

3

The Mechanics of Disposal

Craig Pickering

Introduction

The organization of denationalizations requires a variety of skills. The higher civil service supplies some of these; outside advisers have to be hired to provide others. As denationalizations progress, they throw up a series of issues which these two groups must advise on and which ministers must decide upon. This chapter examines both those who act as 'mechanics' and the issues they encounter. It concentrates on those issues that are most politically significant, in two senses: they may generate a good deal of political controversy, especially in Parliament; alternatively, or in addition, they may have implications for relations between those who organize and those who are organized and their trade unions. The interest to a political scientist of the mechanics of disposal is twofold: their novel features (such as the involvement of merchant banks); and the opportunities they offer to explore some traditional themes in British public administration, such as the influence of civil servants, particularly in areas which can be represented as technical.

This chapter focuses upon the sale of nationalized industries with their staff and resources since May 1979, usually through a flotation on the Stock Exchange. Contracting-out, liberalization, the sale of shares to fund government expenditure (as in the BP sales and the second C&W sale) and other activities which are from time to time labelled as 'privatization' or linked to it are all excluded here. So too are privatizations from the civil service, local government, or the NHS, or any other part of the public sector, though occasional reference is made to the sale of the ROFs because of its similarity in many respects to nationalized industry denationalizations.

The Organizing Institutions

The Centre

The lead in co-ordinating privatization policy was given to the Treasury in

1979. It may be said to be a natural candidate, with its traditional role of controlling public expenditure on nationalized industries ('external finance' in the jargon of public expenditure control). The Department of Industry, as it was in 1979, the Department of Trade and Industry as it is now, might have been chosen. It is a major sponsor of nationalized industries and takes the lead on the Government's policy on industry generally. In a sense, the merger with the Department of Trade in 1983, with the acquisition of responsibility for competition policy, would make such an arrangement more sensible. Though not given the lead, it has continued to play since 1979 a prominent role in administering the policy, centred on its 'own' denationalizations but with an impact on other departments as a source of expertise.

It seems more accurate to characterize the Treasury as co-ordinating privatization rather than directing it. As others have noted, the culture of Whitehall is, within its own walls, one much concerned with persuasion and rationality. Where the relevant Treasury administrative division has interests and views different from those of the department organizing a particular denationalization, it will pursue them with varying degrees of vigour and success. The timing of the conversion of a public corporation into a company under companies legislation provides an example. The Treasury may well be wary of early incorporation, on the grounds that an industry may escape the usual financial controls imposed by central government on nationalized industries (over, for example, their borrowing and their more significant investment decisions). Whilst owned entirely by the Government, the industry cannot be said to be subject to market disciplines to the extent it will be after the sale. But the sponsor department is subject to different pressures on this issue. The urge to establish a record as a new company may count for more than these financial arguments. So there is a balance to be struck, and the sponsor department may well prevail against the Treasury.

Moreover, the Treasury itself is subject to conflicting pressures. On the one hand, denationalization gives rise to the sort of traditional financial concerns just mentioned. In administrative terms, the Treasury will tend to assimilate these into its traditional public expenditure procedures. It may be seen, to that extent, by enthusiasts for privatization as an obstacle to rapid progress. But the Treasury also has a positive role to play. The Government has laid much emphasis on the importance of policies of privatization in its economic policy generally (for example, Moore 1983). This approach may be gathering in force. The Treasury's co-ordinating role gives it a responsibility — and a good position — to try to ensure consistent decisions in particular cases and avoid undesirable precedents, in economic and financial terms. Nevertheless, its success in ensuring consistency has been less than total.

The Cabinet Office will also, as usual, figure at the centre, trying to ensure that ministers are given full opportunity in Cabinet or Cabinet committees to consider policy issues, together and case by case, as they arise. Given the rules on keeping such matters secret, it is impossible to be more specific, but it seems a safe assumption that some such mechanism exists for a policy that has now been conducted for five years. In addition, the Bank of England is kept in close touch with the progress of individual sales. Its main concern is probably the timing of the sale: it will seek the best 'window' between other share issues that are planned or arranged around the time the sale is desired. It also has a watching brief on matters to do with the City. Mr Merlyn Rees, when Labour Shadow Secretary for Energy, suggested that the Bank should take over permanently the functions presently carried out by merchant banks (*Hansard,* 16 March 1982, col. 268) — as it did in a couple of early cases. The suggestion can be ruled out on political grounds: neither the Government, the private sector nor the Bank itself are likely to look on it with favour.

The Department

In specific cases, the sponsor department or the department working on the denationalization of part of itself will be in the lead. It knows most, within central government, about the candidate. And its minister stands to gain or lose most, in political terms, from the outcome. There are various ways of organizing a denationalization: for example, in the case of BAe it was 'steered' by a committee of officials chaired by a junior minister. A policy division may choose to involve interested parties in a less structured way, through *ad hoc* meetings, correspondence and so on. In at least one case, that of the NFC, a working party was set up, comprising the Department of Transport, the industry itself, the merchant bank and solicitors advising the Government, but not the Treasury (though it sometimes attended meetings), reflecting an attitude which has been superseded by the interventionist stance described above. The Treasury would always be represented on such working parties now.

An important point is the extent to which relations between finance divisions and the policy divisions responsible for organizations to be denationalized mirror those between the department and the Treasury. In particular, government departments and their sub-organizations project images which are difficult to define but nonetheless real, though civil servants often play down their significance. Even if such disclaimers are taken at their face value, the different roles of finance and policy divisions are still of administrative significance in so far as they influence the perceptions of others. Nationalized industries, for example, on occasion see policy divisions as their friends and finance divisions as slightly more distanced from their own views on denationalization and the issues it raises. The image of a division or department can also be significant in internal dealings. Like the Treasury, finance divisions can see their colleagues elsewhere in the department as insufficiently interested in the financial implications of a particular policy. By the same logic, policy divisions can perceive their finance colleagues and the Treasury as being too narrow in their concerns. Those concerned with the standard of rural telephone services after BT is sold, for example, may well foresee difficulties in communicating this to colleagues more interested in the financial implications. Such perceptions often do little more than affect the tone of dealings between divisions, but on occasion they have a real effect on the advice given.

Judging by the rank of those who work on denationalizations, departments usually give more weight to the broader questions than to the purely financial ones. An under-secretary from the relevant policy area is usually given the lead and is assisted by the relevant assistant secretary from finance. In the case of NFC, for instance, the Department of Transport gave the major responsibility at working level to the under-secretary from the Freight Directorate and he was assisted by an assistant secretary from the relevant nationalized industries' finance division (McLachlan 1983, 89, confirmed by the Department of Transport). However, as in much to do with Whitehall, it would be wrong to suggest that the roles of policy and finance divisions are clear cut. Both will be aware, to varying degrees, of the other's concerns. There is institutional encouragement to recognize those concerns, but departments are not monoliths: there were differences of view in the Department of Transport, for example, on when NFC should be incorporated. Particularly at the higher grades, from deputy secretary up to permanent secretary, civil servants may have a variety of interests, as part of their formal responsibilities and informally, which they will pursue in the course of their work.

Beyond very occasional meetings, usually at quite a high, even ministerial level, and occasional visits to the industries, Whitehall sees little of the employees of candidate organizations other than senior management. Whatever the merits of such an approach, it is quite clear that it will affect the way in which policy is implemented. For example, arguments about the likelihood of industrial action in particular cases will be filtered through the management of the industry. Civil servants and, through them, ministers will not have a direct source of information about such matters.

Directors, Managers and Professional Advisers

To run the nationalized industries, the Government has often brought in new senior management sympathetic to the policy of denationalization: Sir John (now Lord) King is perhaps the most prominent example. Such individuals are, in their turn, likely to replace less senior staff and introduce changes in the way their businesses are managed. In other cases, such as the NFC and BTDB (renamed ABP), the Government has been content to deal with existing management. Denationalization requires a close working relationship between government and senior management. There are two main reasons for this. First, the Government needs to obtain their co-operation if the denationalization is to go ahead: as demonstrated, for example, by the long delays in selling British Gas's onshore oil property at Wytch Farm, where the Chairman was known to oppose the sale. Second, the Government believes that managers have a right to be consulted on the details of denationalization, if not on whether to proceed in the first place. There is an ironical paradox here, connecting back to earlier discussion of the corporate state: the upper echelons of nationalized industries are integrated into the policy process in order to speed their exclusion from it altogether, or at least to a significant degree. Trade unions and other employees are not involved to anything like the same extent.

Merchant bankers are the professional advisers who seem to merit most attention for a number of reasons. They become highly integrated into the organizational process and advise upon topics which include those which are the most politically controversial, especially in the House of Commons. Moreover, their advice tends to have very important and wide-ranging implications. For example, the ratio of debt to equity concerns both Treasury and department, and the question of whether index-linked pensions will be maintained will influence employee attitudes.

In the cases of NFC and ABP, the same merchant bankers, at least for a time, advised both government department and industry. This unusual practice has not been imitated elsewhere; nowadays, each appoints its own advising bank. In general terms, the role of the department's bank is to advise on how to sell the organization at the best possible price, however defined, from the Government's point of view. The industry's advising bank will represent its interests in the discussions that arise in trying to achieve this end. Though merchant bankers and senior civil servants may often have attended the same schools and universities, and come from similar backgrounds, the two worlds are distinct. Marxists, for example, might assume that a common background would lead to a common view. Such an assumption seems profoundly mistaken. Merchant banks, except in a few specialized fields such as export credit, had little contact with Whitehall before 1979. New jargons must be learned on both sides. Relations between civil servants and merchant bankers depend in part on the rank of the civil servant under consideration. Assistant secretaries and principals may judge a merchant bank primarily by the quantity and quality of the papers it produces. More senior officials may be much more impressed by personal contacts with the senior members of the bank who are handling their particular candidate. In time, the factors which separate the two professions may diminish in importance and almost disappear, but they should not be dismissed.

A few of the major merchant banks have acted as advisers to the Government on the sales of whole enterprises (though others have been involved as advisers to the industries, underwriters, or as advisers on the sale of subsidiaries). Thus, some banks are building up experience. The Ministry of Defence, a newcomer to large-scale denationalization, may have been reassured by Rothschilds' previous experience (despite the outcome of the sales). Table 1 strongly suggests that a bank can build a more permanent relationship with a department, even though it may have to compete for the contract each time.

TABLE 1 Merchant bank advisers to government

Organization	*Government's adviser*	*Department*
Amersham International	Rothschilds	Energy
Associated British Ports	Schroder Wagg	Transport
British Aerospace	Kleinwort Benson	Industry
Britoil	Rothschilds	Energy
Cable & Wireless	Kleinwort Benson	Industry
National Freight Corporation	Schroder Wagg	Transport
Royal Ordnance Factories	Rothschilds	Defence

Share issues also involve accountants, solicitors, firms which specialize in preparing and paying for advertisements of the share issue, and a 'receiving banker' which processes applications for shares. In addition, other merchant banks are involved in the share issue, as issuing houses and underwriters. A major political issue that the involvement of these institutions raises concerns their fees — which the Opposition says are too high. These are not published as a matter of course, but a revealing glimpse was given by Mr John Moore in a Commons debate on AI (*Hansard*, 16 March 1982, col. 296). Underwriters received $1\frac{1}{4}$% of the proceeds of the sale, £800,000; the issuing houses 7/16%, £280,000; and the brokers £80,000. The costs of the whole sale, including the fees of other professional advisers, VAT and stamp duty, were £2.8m. Lord Cockfield gave totals, excluding VAT and stamp duty, of £5m. for BAe, £5.4m. for C&W and £125,000 for NFC (*Hansard*, 1 April 1982, col. 1465). Merchant banks, in contrast, complain that fees are too low and are said to take the work for its prestige (Davis 1983).

Issues

Identifying the Candidates

The selection of nationalized industries as candidates for sale is a highly politicized process. Some have been mentioned in the 1979 and 1983 manifestos; some were suggested by the Conservative Party committee on nationalized industries chaired by Mr Nicholas Ridley (*Economist* 1978); and others have been proposed by individual ministers and MPs (Fowler 1977, Tugendhat 1970). Until the ROFs, civil service denationalizations were so small, in terms of the staff employed and the organizations' turnover, that the service played a much more prominent part in selecting the candidates. Even in the case of the ROFs, the time it took to initiate action suggests that ministers may have given it a low political priority.

The Contents of Legislation

All major denationalizations to date have required or are requiring legislation. The contents of such legislation raise a series of questions. These need to be answered early: the Government either intends to denationalize quickly or, where the prospects are more uncertain, wishes to have the power to be able to take advantage of more favourable economic and financial circumstances. BAe was sold in February 1981 using legislation passed in 1980. Enabling legislation was passed in the same year to cover BA, whose sale is planned for 1985. Cases of the latter variety raise an interesting question — like any enabling legislation not used quickly — as to the propriety of seeking Parliament's agreement to a sale so far in advance: should the Government not wait until Parliament has a better idea of the circumstances under which the firm is likely to be sold? The Government might with justice reply that it always intends to sell early, but sometimes the market turns against its plans. The legislation might have effect for a limited period: alternatively, the Government might get candidates further down the road to sale before proposing legislation.

The major objects of legislation are to provide powers to sell the organization in question, or its subsidiaries, or both, and to get it or them into a legal and financial form which eases the sale. For AI and C&W, already equity-based companies, no further powers, other than the first, were needed. More usually, candidates have to be converted from public corporations into companies with shares. The opportunity may also be taken to reduce an organization's debts to ease sale. At incorporation, debts are usually extinguished and exchanged for equity, though the legislation usually leaves the Secretary of State and the Treasury with a free hand on valuing the equity. Denationalization legislation does not experiment in company organization. The Government has throughout been content to follow the traditional model of company usually found in the private sector.

There are several interesting variations between Acts. The consent of the Treasury was not needed to sell AI or BR's subsidiaries, though no doubt in practice it was or would be consulted. Some legislation, such as that covering Britoil, provides for employee share schemes, whereas the legislation covering BAe and the NFC, where such schemes were nonetheless used, does not. This omission is particularly notable in the second case, because the company was eventually bought by the employees, led by their senior management. For BAe and BA, the device was adopted of a target investment limit, a limit upon the percentage of shares with voting rights which the Government might hold after the initial sale of shares. This limit can only be revised downwards and must not be transgressed except in exceptional circumstances. It is difficult to see why this device was not used in other cases, such as ABP, where the Government intended to retain a minority shareholding. The only personnel matter frequently covered is pension provision, and not all statutes mention it. For BAe, ABP and BA, service in the old organization counts for the purpose of calculating pension rights in the new organization; but for others no such powers were taken. The legislation covering NFC took the opportunity to fund deficiencies in that firm's pension funds (£47m. out of the proceeds of the sale of £53m.). Some legislative provisions appear entirely declaratory in nature, particularly many of those relating to ABP.[1]

The legislative provisions common to most denationalizations are found as early as 1972, in the legislation which provided for the sale of Thomas Cook. The differences discussed above suggest that, though the legislation sometimes varies for good reason, on other occasions there is a lack of consistency in the organization of denationalizations. So the inconsistencies in government policy referred to by Steel (1984) begin very early on, at the time the legislation is drafted. No doubt provisions are borrowed and some expertise is passed on, particularly within individual departments, but there has also been a good deal of leeway to legislate for individual cases as the minister, his civil servants and the Treasury judge fit.

It is also noteworthy that the legislation leaves a good deal to be settled administratively. Such questions as government's relations with the industry after incorporation and sale, the size of the residual government shareholding, and the method of sale are not covered in the legislation. It can sometimes be argued, on the price to be sought, for example, that the Government should not tie its own hands unduly to get the best possible deal, however defined, for the taxpayer. But on some issues, such as the method of sale to be chosen, Parliament gets no opportunity to discuss them early enough to affect the decision. Judging by the interest it shows after the event, such opportunities would be welcomed. The controversy over the price obtained for AI, in the light of share price movements immediately after the sale, provides an example. If Parliament had debated the method of sale during the passage of the Atomic Energy (Miscellaneous Provisions) Act 1981, some of the heat might have been removed from the post-mortem debate. No doubt there would still have been complaints from the Opposition, but their case could have been assessed in the light of points made without the benefit of hindsight.

Form of the Sale

A major question on form is whether to sell the organization as a whole or part by part. Generally, the Government's preference is for the former, apparently on political rather than financial grounds. Employees and Conservative backbenchers support this approach. In profitable concerns, there is no necessary conflict between financial and political pressures. But NFC seems a good test of the Government's preferences in this area. Though the option of selling its profitable subsidiaries was never absolutely ruled out, the bulk of the Department of Transport's efforts was directed at selling the entire firm as a going concern. The Government only seems willing to make state-owned enterprises sell subsidiaries where the main business, as in BGC, is a monopoly, or, like BL, is impossible to sell in the short term at what the Government and Parliament would regard as a reasonable price.

Financial Issues

As already noted, one step sometimes taken is to improve the candidate's balance sheet. The Government wrote off £100m. of NFC's debts and over £80m. of the BTDB's. In each case, the debt was replaced by equity, though not of equal nominal value. The need to fund NFC's pension fund deficiencies also has to be remembered. The write-offs must also be assessed in the light of the history of nationalized industry financing, a rather unhappy one from the taxpayer's and the Treasury's point of view. Though it is not an argument that applies with equal force in all cases, it can be said that write-offs might well have happened anyway, albeit at a different time. There are clearly rather complicated judgements to be made here, with a good deal of room for manoeuvre by the various interests at work on advising on the appropriate capital structures.

Where incorporation as a company under companies legislation is necessary, an important issue is the timing. There is not much in the way of case law, but enough to show that practice varies. BAe and ABP were set up in their new corporate form a matter of weeks before the sale of shares to the general public, whereas NFC operated as a 100% government-owned company for 16 months, and would have done so for longer if the management had not taken the initiative to organize the buy-out. The first two cases no doubt represent the Government's ideal, and were possible because both companies were easily marketable. NFC, with a long history of poor profitability, and even loss-making, was much less plausible. The thought behind early incorporation was that the company would be better placed to establish a track record in the eyes of the market as a company cut off from the sources of finance open to a nationalized industry. The theory was never put to the test, since there was no sale to the general public. BA was incorporated on 1 April 1984, with a view to sale early in 1985; but the Secretary of State was careful to point out that 'broadly' similar financial controls could continue until then. The next denationalization that will raise this issue will be the ROFs, where incorporation is planned (for October 1984) well before private capital is brought in. The form of the latter has not even been decided. As well as the views of the Treasury and sponsor departments discussed above, the issue engages the candidate and its advisers. Senior management of NFC were keen to be incorporated early, apparently for the same reasons as the Department of Transport wished them to be. The Ministry of Defence and management at ROFs are likely to have pointed to the last two years' surpluses as grounds for early incorporation, with the Treasury, more cautious, remembering a deficit in 1980-81. It is perhaps significant as an indication of his priorities that the Chief Executive's Statement in the 1982-83 Annual Report only mentions incorporation and not denationalization (ROFs 1983, 2 and 28).

NFC yields little in the way of general lessons on relations between the industry and government during incorporation before sale. It did not encounter any great commercial difficulties that would have necessitated urgent injections of finance in that period. The major concern in its dealings with the Department of Transport was the organization of the buy-out, wasted experience to the extent that the Government has not considered that model elsewhere.

Broadly speaking, the Government has two main options for the method of sale, an offer at a fixed price or by tender (though there are others, such as placing by private treaty). In the former, all those who wish to buy at the stated price are sold shares, scaled down in proportion to total bids in the event of over-subscription. In the latter, the Government on advice announces a striking price, and all those who have tendered above that are sold shares, at that price.Setting aside the financial implications of the two methods, one political factor which is important is that the tender method is thought to deter small investors, since they have to make a judgement about the striking price. So the bulk of sales of public enterprises have been at a fixed price (though the second C&W and ABP sales suggest that the tender method is becoming more popular). But ministers have some room for manoeuvre. Mr Nigel Lawson, as Secretary of State for Energy, long an advocate of the tender method, sought to overcome this supposed political disadvantage in the Britoil sale by allowing small investors simply to say they wanted to buy at the striking price, whatever it turned out to be. He was perhaps encouraged to adopt this method by the criticisms he had incurred over the massive over-subscription for AI, at a fixed price. In the event, 99% of Britoil shares were sold to small shareholders (holding 2,000 shares or less) and employees.

This proportion was so high because of the circumstances of the sale which made it so politically controversial. Britoil was massively under-subscribed — by about 70% — probably because last-minute developments in the oil market made institutions unwilling to buy. The Opposition made much of this under-subscription, just as they had, for the opposite reason, attacked the AI, C&W and BAe issues. There is a good deal of rhetoric in the Opposition's stance. It is a fair point that fixing a selling price is a very inexact science, and that most issues are under or over-subscribed. But Mr Lawson seems on weak ground in making this point about Britoil (*Hansard*, 22 November 1982, cols. 598-599). There must be limits to the extent to which judgements on the sale price can err, if professional advice is worth taking. A similar question has been raised by both the opposition and the PAC about the value of underwriting (PAC 1982).

Underwriters' commissions are larger than any other advisers' fees and critics see them as an unnecessary expense; they are a form of insurance and governments do not usually insure. Moreover, it is thought wrong to give those who advise on the price a financial interest in the sale. The Government's reply is that in under-subscribed cases like Britoil, only underwriting can take the organization into the private sector to the desired extent.

Special treatment for employees in share sales has been the rule in nationalized industry denationalizations and a feature to which ministers seem to attach much importance. Employees are offered free shares, and may be given £ for £ matching offers and preference in the ordinary share sale. The first two are financed by the Government rather than their employers. Total employee shareholdings immediately after sale are, with the dramatic exception of NFC, usually a very small minority, often of the order of 2-3% of total ordinary shares. Take up, as one would expect given the free offer, is very high, of the order of 80-90%. It is more surprising that some employees do not want even the free shares. For small investors, the Government's formula is that, in fixed price sales, it takes into account its objective of wider share ownership when considering applications to buy shares. In the Britoil sale, shares were to be paid for in two instalments, to encourage small investors. An estimated 22.6% of AI's shares were taken up by small investors (see, for example, *Hansard*, 16 March 1982, col. 296) and around 19% for ABP. Such investors may often hold shares for only a short time. *Labour Research* points out that 1200 ABP accounts were closed in 4 months: 1.8m. shares (about 9% of the total) were sold.[2] These figures suggest severe limits to the extent to which denationalization can widen share ownership.

This encouragement to employees and small investors to hold shares sits rather uneasily with the Government's stated preference for the free market, since it involves administrative interference in the sale to produce a desired political result. In the case of the free share offers for employees, there is also a conflict, albeit quite a small one, with the objective of achieving the best price for the taxpayer. Both policies have the advantage of broadening political support for the denationalization, though probably not sufficiently to impede Labour attempts to renationalize, mainly because of the small proportion of shares held by these groups.

The Government must itself also decide whether or not to retain a shareholding. It does not seem to have pursued a grand design: it makes up its mind on the circumstances of particular cases, and is careful never to close its options prematurely. In the 1984 Budget debate, Mr Peter Rees, the Chief Secretary to the Treasury, announced the Government's intentions of selling, in due course, all of its current residual shareholdings (Rees 1984). Even with an industry like NFC, which it said openly was not appropriate for the public sector, the Government left itself the option of retaining a minority shareholding until quite late in the day. That said, purely commercial undertakings, as the Government perceives them, are likely to be sold outright. Majority shareholdings have in the end always been ruled out, except for C&W, though the option was also publicly contemplated for BAe. The main pressure here is that a majority shareholding would mean that the organization concerned would continue to be classified, for various purposes, as part of the public sector. A mixture of motives is at work in deciding whether to retain a minority shareholding, with defence industries like BAe and the ROFs being obvious candidates. On occasion, there are thought to be commercial advantages. For example, C&W does a good deal of business with foreign governments. It was argued at the time of the first sale that they would be less willing to do business with a completely privately-owned company. The second sale of C&W shares in November 1983 suggests that this argument may diminish in force with time. The firm's results since denationalization seem to give shareholders no grounds for concern. Finally, the Government's intention to retain a minority shareholding in BT suggests that firms that have a strategic role in the economy, and are monopolies in at least a significant part of their operations, may be candidates for such treatment. In our political culture there may be a need to express the state's involvement in such industries through a shareholding, even when the government of the day espouses a free market ideology.

Personnel Issues

As noted above, the personnel implications of nationalized industry denationalizations tend to be dealt with 'in-house' and are thus beyond the scope of this chapter, except in so far as they attract parliamentary interest. Even as dramatic an instance as the POEU's opposition to the sale of BT is treated, in public at least, as a matter for the industry rather than the Government.The main personnel issues which seem to receive most parliamentary attention are pay levels, pension arrangements and job security. That they receive such attention is attributable to a number of influences. First, the vacuum left by the shortage of information on the financial side can be filled by discussion of personnel issues, where dealings between ministers and (more usually) managers on the one hand and trade union officials and employees on the other produce a good deal of material. Secondly, the Parliamentary Labour Party includes among its ranks a number of spokesmen for trade unions which represent nationalized industry employees. Thirdly, MPs from all the major political parties have constituency interests in organizations that are candidates for sale. The ROFs are an excellent example, with 11 factories spread around the country. Fourthly, Conservative backbenchers seem to like to argue that employees should gain from denationalization, through their employer's freedom to operate more commercially. The Government appears to have been very successful in its refusal to make any commitments on these issues to the employees of nationalized industries that have been sold. Even in the case of ROFs, the only commitment the Government has had to make concerns the pensions of existing employees.

Pensions can also provide a rough measure of the Government's political commitment to privatization. The maximum cost of transferring ROFs' employees' 'accrued rights' (as benefits already paid for are called in pensions jargon) to the new pensions scheme is estimated at around £250m. The Government points out that, over time, this expenditure, on certain actuarial assumptions, would have been incurred anyway; but its commitment hinges on the fact that it has decided to bear this cost in the near future rather than spreading it over many years, during most of which the individual ministers concerned will not be in their current posts.

Conclusion

The mechanics of disposal bear little resemblance to those of car engines. No diagram showing how to organize disposals can be displayed that much resembles those that figure in car manuals, no matter how much political scientists and some of those who work on or are affected by denationalizations might desire one. Yet certain themes emerge. For the political scientist, there is a glimpse of the complicated structures of views and interests in Whitehall departments and their sub-departments: an odd mixture of co-ordination and inconsistency in organizing policy. It is a world that has practices of its own, which can accommodate other institutions but does so selectively. No general theory of policy-making in British government can be constructed from studying the mechanics of disposal, but certain questions are raised which might fruitfully be asked elsewhere about, for instance, the roles and images of government departments and, more particularly, the nature of relationships between central departments and others, such as merchant banks. The existing literature leaves much scope for additional research. For those interested in gleaning practical lessons about denationalization, the main ones are perhaps the need for better co-ordination within government and greater attempts to involve employees, trade unions (if they can be persuaded to co-operate) and any others who wish to make a contribution in organizing disposals. Greater consistency and clarity of purpose — while recognizing that every sale throws up some unique issues — seem required. There is a need to improve the quality of public debate on the mechanics of disposals. Steel (1984, 97) has suggested a White Paper, greater parliamentary interest and possibly legislation. General enabling legislation to provide answers to the questions every denationalization must face, with shorter Acts to deal with the unique circumstances of individual cases, would be one possible approach. Another would be a review of the policy to date, with recommendations for the future, by the Treasury and Civil Service Committee. Though the programme cannot be started anew, the experience gained to date might usefully be distilled.

NOTES

1 For example, it may operate harbours, provide port facilities and, in effect, through one sub-section, whatever its board judges it fit to do. It may charge and borrow as it sees fit, subject to other legislation. It has a duty to provide port facilities it thinks expedient. Most notably, '... in the performance of its functions Associated British Ports shall have regard to the interests in general of its employees and the employees of its subsidiaries' (Transport Act 1981, Section 9). In fairness, it has to be said that other major commercial harbours are usually similarly treated in legislation.

2 Extracted from figures published in Hansard (16 February 1983, col. 75) and *Labour Research* (1983). The Department of Industry told the PAC that the number of shareholders, other than employees, holding less than 1,000 shares fell from 149,302 immediately after flotation to 23,042 less than a year later. In contrast, there was only one shareholder holding 1m. or more, other than the Government, immediately after flotation, but 13 after the same interval (PAC 1982, 15).

4

The Union Response to Denationalization

David Thomas

It is also hard to see how a policy of outright sale of the entire Corporation could be compatible with the over-riding need of any government to achieve some kind of *modus vivendi* with the trade unions.

Internal memorandum, written in March 1979, by Gerry Flanagan, planning director of the NFC, quoted in McLachlan 1983, 15.

Union Interest in Denationalization

Mr Flanagan, like many people at the time, misjudged the new Conservative Party. The Government has not only rejected the previous consensus on the nationalized industries and the unions, but it has linked the two issues together. For ministers, the power given to unions by public ownership is part of the problem of nationalization. 'Public sector trade unions have been extraordinarily successful in gaining advantages for themselves in the pay hierarchy by exploiting their monopoly collective bargaining position', as the Financial Secretary to the Treasury has put it (Moore 1983).

Unions have both practical and ideological reasons for resisting denationalization. They were central to the debate which preceded the Attlee nationalizations (Weiner 1960). They were key participants in the few recent cases of nationalization (see, for example, the report which prefigured the nationalization of shipbuilding : Labour Party-TUC-CSEU 1972). And the nationalization statutes often required management to recognize and consult unions, and to promote collective bargaining. So it is not surprising that unions have won clear benefits from public ownership.

In 1980, more than 90% of white collar and manual workers in nationalized industries were in unions; in private manufacturing, 75% of manual workers and a mere 39% of white collar workers were unionized. In the nationalized sector, management recognized manual unions in 98% of establishments and white collar unions in 94%; the corresponding figures for private manufacturing were 68% and 32%. Among manual workers in the nationalized industries, 72% were in a closed shop, compared with less than half in the private sector (Daniel and Millward 1983).

There is evidence too — though more controversial and uncertain — that nationalized industry workers are pace-setters in wage rises (Foster, Henry and Trinder 1984; Heald 1983, 221-226; though see Zabalza 1984 for a contrary view). This was most noticeable in the 1970s, when the turbulent pay bargaining in the nationalized industries contributed to the general crisis of the public sector (Heald 1983, chap.9; Winchester 1983). Their pay bargaining is highly centralized, with few important negotiations at plant level (Daniel and Millward 1983, 188), a factor which moulds the style of their industrial relations and channels power in nationalized industry unions towards the most senior national officials.

Given their historical, ideological and practical attachment to nationalization, unions have been singularly unsuccessful in countering denationalization. They came nowhere near deflecting any of the asset sales completed by the first Thatcher Government, even though some — like the BTDB — were traditional centres of union power. Only in one case — gas showrooms — could a strong case be made for union action having helped to thwart a proposed sale, though the steel unions also claimed credit for the collapse of the proposed US-Ravenscraig link (*Morning Star*, 28 December 1983).

This is not to say that denationalization has been trouble-free. The 1979 manifesto pledge to sell BS is still unhonoured. Other sales have been protracted affairs; but the delays have been due to the recession, not to union opposition. If a medal were struck for defence of the public sector, it would belong, not to militant unions, but to the board of BGC for their epic manoeuvres over Wytch Farm.

This chapter concentrates on 'denationalization' — the sale of assets in traditional nationalized industries and Company Act companies. Denationalization is a central part of the Government's privatization programme which also encompasses 'liberalization' — the introduction of more competition into the nationalized sector. So far, liberalization has had a major impact in the bus and civil aviation industries, a moderate impact in telecommunications, and a minor impact in some other industries like post, gas and electricity. Liberalization has forced enterprises like the NBC and BA to cut back their least used, less profitable services and concentrate on their more profitable operations. As such, liberalization poses similar problems for nationalized industry unions as the recession has posed for unions throughout the economy. The main difference is that liberalization usually requires legislation, which allows unions to oppose it during the legislative process.

Denationalization will remain at the top of the political agenda. The candidates for partial or total sale mentioned either in the last Parliament (Howe 1981), the 1983 manifesto or in this Parliament (Moore 1983) now cover almost every nationalized industry. The unions believe that the influence of the Government's wish to sell the public sector is even more pervasive. On this view, it has been the over-riding objective which has determined the industries' path since 1979. Thus, the financial turnaround which the Government has demanded of the industries is a prologue to denationalization. It has entailed major redundancies in the loss-making enterprises. Liberalization is another spur to privatization: it forces public corporations to become more efficient, thus making them more attractive to buyers; and it helps meet the charge that denationalization means the transfer of monopoly from the public to the private sector. Fashionable management tactics like decentralization aid denationalization by hindering cross-subsidies and facilitating the piecemeal sale of a corporation (see the NUM's 1983 comment on MMC 1983).

This view — widely held in the union movement — is, however, too broad. Some of these policies, like the financial squeeze, might have been followed by a government uninterested in selling assets. This chapter takes a narrower focus. What have unions done *before* denationalization in the corporations that have been sold in whole or in part, and in those industries (like BT) where it is a live issue? What have unions done *after* denationalization in those enterprises which have been sold? The broad answers are nicely double-edged. The unions have failed to stop sales, but they have achieved many of their subsidiary bargaining objectives. After denationalization, the first results are opposite to what would be implied by the thesis that public ownership boosts union power.

Union Response Before Denationalization

Spreading the Word

Faced with the threat of denationalization the least a union can do is to lobby influential groups, and to try to win public opinion against the sale. Lobbies of Parliament, delegations to ministers, press briefings, special conferences of members and of other sympathetic groups, and reams of publicity material — these are routine union responses.

Whilst of itself this activity is uninteresting, it means that denationalization has had two, presumably unintended, consequences. First, unions have drawn even closer to the Labour Party. They have been in close touch with Opposition spokesmen, particularly at committee stage, on specific issues like pensions rights. Second, unions have developed more professional press and publicity capabilities, having in the past been a byword for amateurishness.

The most professional campaign has been run by the telecommunications unions against the privatization of BT (POEU 1984). The POEU and the BTUC have taken on extra staff, hired media consultants and spent some £1½m. in about 18 months. The campaign material has varied in sophistication and targeting. Much of it, including a special video, has been aimed at the unions' own members. Target campaigns were launched in marginal constituencies during the 1983 election. The unions have issued pamphlets directed at special groups: rural communities; the poor; the blind and disabled; consumers; trade unionists; and British business. They commissioned an American consultant's report on telecommunications liberalization in the United States (BTUC 1983). They have advertised in the local and national press, and were prepared to spend £¼m. on television advertisements, but the IBA rejected their request as 'political' (*Labour Weekly*, 10 February 1984). Opinion polls conducted by Gallup in December 1982 and November 1983 showed a movement in public opinion against the BT sale, but it is impossible to know whether this was due to the unions' campaign. At the very least, however, it must have raised public awareness about the complex issues involved in selling BT. It may also have contributed to assurances given by the Government about the position of special groups, like rural inhabitants and the blind.

Looking for Friends

Unions have been careful to build alliances against denationalization. The POEU's campaign, as already noted, has been aimed at distinct sections of the population. The gas unions cultivated consumer groups when opposing the sale of gas showrooms in 1981 (Lord 1983). The unions' attempts to win over consumer opinion, however, have been hindered by the fact that consumer groups are often weak and suspicious of public sector unions.

A useful group for unions to win over are the corporations' top management. It is excellent publicity if a board states openly that denationalization would damage its enterprise. In the early days, such utterances were not uncommon. The BAe board issued a statement in August 1979 stressing 'the uncertainty and distraction of changes effected by parliament'. Lord Kearton, BNOC Chairman, described the sale of its oil and gas interests as a 'bad business decision' (*Financial Times,* 1 September 1979). Robert Atkinson, BS Chairman, said there would be board resignations if the warship yards were sold separately (*Financial Times*, 6 August 1980). Atkinson for one mentioned union pressure as a factor in talking of resignations. But the Government closed this potentially fruitful channel for union lobbying by appointing supporters of denationalization when board vacancies arose.

At the TUC level, the unions tried to enlist the support of the Nationalised Industries' Chairmen's Group (TUC 1980, 271). The NICG expressed concern at any fragmentation of the industries which might result from sales, but would not be drawn on the basic issue. After that, the TUC stressed the more oblique theme that the public and private sectors were interdependent. The TUC conceived such ideas as part of a long-term struggle against new orthodoxies, like privatization (TUC 1981a, 276 and 294). At the depth of the recession, stressing 'interdependence' was a thinly disguised call for a public investment led reflation. This struck a receptive chord in the NICG. Both the TUC and the NICG pushed the issue at the National Economic Development Council (NICG 1981; NEDO 1981), though without any apparent impact on the Government.

As the failure of such conventional alliances became clear, the TUC was forced back to basics. This took the form of arguing for the necessity of public provision across the whole of the public sector — nationalized industries and public services (TUC 1983, 267). More recently, the TUC has published more aggressive material designed to undermine privatization by highlighting factors like the underpricing of public assets (see the anti-privatization material published by the TUC on 12 March 1984). It was pushed this way partly by certain unions, like the POEU which moved a resolution at the 1983 Congress demanding a TUC-led campaign in defence of the public sector, and partly by a growing awareness in the unions of the low esteem in which the nationalized industries are held.

Changing the Line

Unions have adopted new policies which they hoped would help avert denationalization. Two examples will be given, a 'hard' and a 'soft' one. Firstly, if the Labour Party were committed to renationalizing corporations without compensation, then investors would not buy shares in those corporations. That was the view of many unions. Traditionally moderate unions like the ISTC, TSSA and the Boilermakers spoke in favour of no compensation resolutions which were carried at TUC Congresses and Labour Party Conferences after 1979.

The policy had no effect even on the early sales (like BAe) which were completed when the Government was doing badly in the polls and even though it was noted in several denationalization prospectuses. It was ineffective because it was incredible; and it immediately brought reservations from the TUC General Council about its implications for shareholdings held by employees, pension funds and foreigners (TUC 1979, 610). All denationalization share issues, bar one, were heavily over-subscribed. The exception, Britoil, was launched *after* the TUC and Labour Party had abandoned the policy at their 1982 Conferences. So incredible was the idea that one union which was party to it, the NUR, itself bought shares in a denationalized asset, the Gleneagles Hotels Group.

The sole impact of the no compensation policy was to embarrass the Labour Party. By 1982, with an election in sight, this albatross could no longer be ignored. The TUC-Labour Party Liaison Committee drew up a statement changing the policy to one of 'no speculative gain' (Labour Party-TUC-CSEU 1982). This too had no impact on the sales. But it can be judged successful to the extent that Labour's opponents failed to make capital out of it during the 1983 election campaign, which was its purpose.

Secondly, the TUC adopted a policy of a quite different kind, one of whose aims was to head off denationalization. In 1981, there was widespread debate about the industries having access to the private capital markets to finance profitable investment. The TUC published a paper (TUC 1981b) which concluded that 'the nationalised industries, like their EEC counterparts, should be free to issue bonds to the general public and raise loans in all appropriate ways on the capital markets'. This was a departure in Labour movement thinking, which had previously accepted uncritically National Loans Fund arrangements. The TUC felt sufficiently nervous about it to underline that it remained 'totally opposed to privatisation' (TUC 1981a, 295).

The TUC was party to the Treasury-NICG-CBI-TUC report on nationalized industries' investment (NEDC 1981), which discussed 'hybrid' projects owned by the public sector and financed by the private sector. As with 'interdependence', the unions formed an easy alliance with the NICG on 'hybridity'. Both wanted to increase the investment funds available to the industries through this route.

Additionally, the TUC backed the idea because 'in the current circumstances of some nationalised industries, bonds were an alternative to privatisation' (TUC 1982, 275). The NEDC report had said that direct access to risk capital should be allowed only if it improved efficiency by introducing private sector disciplines: hence the notion of a 'performance bond'. The unions thought this half-way house to denationalization might be acceptable to the Government; the telecommunications unions were particularly keen on the 'Buzby bond'. In the end, though, the idea came to nothing. An opportunity was missed to supply public corporations with limited amounts of extra capital in return for commitments from management and unions to improve efficiency.

Pulling Out the Troops

Few unions have used their strongest sanction, industrial action, against denationalization. Yet the most substantial analysis to date of a particular sale (McLachlan 1983) underlines the vulnerability of a public corporation in metamorphosis. City and management opinion was very nervous about the novelty of the NFC buy-out and the impact of the recession. Well-timed industrial disruption might have sunk the flotation.

There have been few strikes of any size against privatization. Unions in the gas industry, the ROFs and Sealink have carried out token stoppages. The gas unions' action was probably the most successful (Lord 1983). In 1981, they held a one-day strike against the proposed sale of the gas showrooms. It was only a token stoppage, though the unions were threatening further action. Yet in the autumn of 1981 the Government rescinded its decision. The strong doubts voiced by the BGC, consumer groups and appliance manufacturers must have weighed with the Government; but so too, one supposes, must the readiness to strike of the traditionally moderate gas unions. For their part, the unions motivated their members because of fears that the sale would have a quick impact on jobs.

The POEU has waged by far the most extensive campaign of industrial action against privatization (both denationalization, the sale of BT, and liberalization, in the guise of Mercury). Between August and November 1983, the union took action against BT's rival, Mercury; Mercury's parent companies; City and government targets; and the international exchanges. The action included strikes, work to rules, the blacking of maintenance and the refusal to interconnect Mercury. The union spent over £3m. on the action, partly financed by a £1 a week levy on members working normally (POEU 1984).

BT responded by 'bussing in' engineers to exchanges in dispute, and by suspending or sacking POEU members who were working to rule, striking or refusing to cross picket lines. In November, Mercury secured an injunction under the 1982 Employment Act against the POEU's refusal to interconnect it. BT warned that this made legal action by its board a stronger possibility (*Financial Times*, 18 November 1983). By early December, the POEU acknowledged defeat by returning its members to work.

The POEU's conduct of the dispute will remain controversial. It was tactically correct to focus the action. It aimed at business traffic and companies involved in privatization, knowing that it would be counter-productive to inconvenience the public. Its shock troops were therefore in the inner London branches most likely to take action. The small number of members involved (2-3,000) allowed the union to pay those on strike or suspended average take-home pay.

However the union displayed fatally poor tactics in other respects. First, the POEU overestimated the speed with which its action would bite. Mercury told the High Court that the action had cost it £1½m. (*Financial Times*, 18 October 1983), but its impact in other areas was not great. Second, paying those on strike or suspended average take-home pay was overgenerous: it drained the union's finances, especially since management began to court suspensions at the international exchanges and since the levy was under-subscribed (*Financial Times*, 22 December 1983). Third, Mercury's successful court action, coupled with BT's threat of litigation, damaged the union's morale: like the rest of the union movement, the POEU had no credible strategy to counteract the Government's industrial relations legislation. The Mercury decision appears to jeopardize any industrial action against privatization, though the law is evolving almost from case to case and it was not evoked against later strikes at the ROFs and Sealink.

Fourth, and most important, the basic objectives were badly thought out.

The union voiced only one aim: to force the Government to withdraw the Telecommunications Bill and abandon the sale of BT. It appeared to have no fall-back position at the time, even though it pursued the kind of subsidiary objectives described in the next section once the industrial action had collapsed. Given this Government's political psychology, there was never any chance of it securing its basic aim. To compound matters, the action was badly timed: a union just might disrupt a sale by sustained industrial action in the weeks before flotation, but not during the early stages of the parliamentary procedure.

Making the Best of a Bad Job

Normally, however, unions are nothing if not flexible. They have demonstrated their ultimate pragmatism by at times accepting denationalization as the lesser of two evils, when the alternative was complete closure of an enterprise or plant. The ISTC was ready to see Shotton hived off, rather than closed as an integrated works (*Financial Times*, 9 February 1980). Unions accepted the merger of the private Hoverlloyd and BR's Hovercraft, because they doubted Hovercraft's independent viability (MMCa 1981). Unions backed the buy-out of Tyne Shiprepair rather than see it close (*Financial Times*, 25 January 1984). And similarly with Scott Lithgow, private ownership was an offer the unions could hardly refuse when the only alternative was closure.

In more typical examples, unions have adopted two subsidiary bargaining objectives. First, they have wanted public corporations to pass into the private sector intact. The unions sought assurances on this in three companies to be denationalized which had distinct subsidiaries or production units with variable profit levels: the NFC, the BTDB, and BAe where AUEW-TASS was worried that the Dynamics Group would be sold separately. None of these was fragmented on privatization. On the other hand, BNOC, where union influence was weak, was split in two. Equally the sale of BSC, BL and BR subsidiaries can be interpreted as fragmentation before the sale of the main business.

Second, unions have wanted guarantees that their members' jobs and terms and conditions would be unaffected. It is central to the concept of denationalization — a return to market disciplines — that such guarantees are impossible. The Transfer of Undertakings Regulations are the main legal provisions governing terms and conditions on transfer of ownership, though the courts have not ruled definitively on whether they apply to denationalizations. They imply only that the new owner takes over the terms and conditions existing on denationalization: thereafter, however, the new owner can open renegotiations (Hepple 1982).

Nevertheless, pensions have to be considered before denationalization. Many public sector schemes are index-linked and substantially in deficit. Few private buyers would take that on. The Government, eager to sell, has an interest in ending index-linking and in seeing to proper funding. The unions also want proper funding, but in addition to retain the best possible benefits.

Pensions negotiations before denationalization have been varied and horrendously complex. In one case, BAe, there was no real problem since there was no index-linking. In others, the Government paid heavily to ensure that the pensions issue was not a blockage: four-fifths of the money from selling the NFC found its way back to the pension fund and the resulting pension settlement was generous (McLachlan 1983, chap.8). In yet others, management moved decisively to end index-linking even before the sale of a corporation (BA statement, 25 January 1984). But given that it was unrealistic to try to keep index-linking, unions have in general negotiated good pension settlements, especially for existing employees. If there are exceptions to that generalization, they are in peripheral areas, like the BR hotels and former BSC subsidiaries like Redpath Dorman Long (on the latter, see TUC 1982, 318; TUC 1983, 310). The steel unions complained to the Industry and Trade Committee about the pensions implications of previous denationalizations; as a result, this all-party committee recommended that future spin-offs from BSC should involve adequate provision for pensions (Industry and Trade Committee 1983, para 34 and Qs 114 and 122).

A striking example of a union receiving assurances before a sale is a letter dated 4 November 1983 from BT's board member for personnel to the general secretary of the POEU. With varying degrees of firmness, the letter assures the POEU about foreign takeover, excessive price rises for domestic customers, the run-down of rural services and non-domestic services like kiosks, the abandonment of emergency services, the splitting and piecemeal sale of the corporation, and the implications for POEU members' jobs, pay, conditions of employment and pensions (see also BTUC 1984 for the unions' assessment of what their campaign achieved).

Some items on which unions have sought assurances — like the foreign takeovers of BAe and BT — the Government had no intention of allowing in the first place. Others, like keeping the corporations intact, are goals shared by management. It is also arguable that assurances given to unions, like those in the BT letter just mentioned, have been couched in such general and qualified terms as to be worthless: management will always be able to say that they have been nullified by circumstances. Yet it is unlikely that the unions' efforts have accounted for nothing: at the very least, they have helped furnish unions with a platform of expectations from which to defend their members' interests after denationalization.

Unions Change Too

The run-up to denationalization has brought contradictory pressures to bear on unions. Their final significance is unclear. Two examples have already been noted: some unions have improved their lobbying and publicity and have drawn even closer to the Labour Party.

Preparing for denationalization has strained some already fragile inter-union relations. The NFC unions held different views on the buy-out, ranging from the TGWU which campaigned for its members not to buy shares to URTU which explained the scheme and its objectives in its journal. The TSSA and the MNAOA had to withdraw their support from some of the publicity material issued by the Sealink unions against Sealink's sale because it went too far for their tastes in condemning the NFC buy-out.

Conversely, the UCW's support (including a £½m. donation) for the POEU in the autumn 1983 dispute has improved traditionally prickly POEU-UCW relations. Similarly, the CPSA's backing helped smooth the way for the merger of the CPSA's post and telecom members with the POEU. The TGWU's national secretary for the docks has told the author that denationalization has drawn the unions closer together in ABP, where union relations have often been difficult.

Denationalization has also fostered militancy in normally quiet unions. The POEU, traditionally moderate and unused to industrial action, is an example. Though the union has been slowly moving left for almost a decade, anger about the sale of BT contributed in 1983 to the left's capture of the executive for the first time since 1948 (Batstone, Ferner and Terry 1984, 237ff.).

Privatization, coupled with the Government's views of public sector managers, has had an effect on the small management unions in the nationalized industries like the STE, EMA, BACM, and SIMA. High union densities in managerial and professional grades are a special case of the high union densities among white collar staff in general in the nationalized industries, which has already been noted (Heald 1983, 217-8). Squeezed between senior management and the clerical and manual unions, the relations of the specialist unions with other sections of the workforce are under strain, as when STE members were pressed to do POEU work in the international exchanges in autumn 1983. The general secretary of the ultra-moderate EMA has warned that a sale of the electricity supply industry might be met with industrial action (*Financial Times*, 19 April 1984). These unions' traditionally non-political outlook is also under threat. The STE's membership even voted to set up a political fund in 1983. This trend could catch on if the Trade Union Act means that unions' publicity against privatization will have to come from their political funds, as ministers have suggested (*Financial Times*, 2 March 1984).

Some unions have adjusted their structures as the corporations have reorganized before denationalization. The POEU used to negotiate for members on the same grade across BT, the PO and National Girobank. Now it has three separate negotiations. Faced with quicker management decision-taking and decentralization in BT, the POEU's national executive has reorganized its committee structure to speed up its decisions and give a bit more power to its regions.

The run-up to denationalization is bringing another change in unions which could turn out to be the most important of all. Many public sector unions are industrial unions of sorts: they have restricted their attentions to public sector workers within their industrial sphere of influence. That self-denying ordinance cannot continue if public monopolies are sold and liberalized. NALGO (which organizes white collar staff in gas, electricity, water and buses) has agreed a rule change so that it can recruit workers in the private sector. The POEU changed its rules to allow recruitment outside its traditional areas in 1981. The bracing wind of competition could sweep through the unions, as well as the corporations. ASTMS is seeking recognition in Mercury: if BT is sold, if Mercury is a success, and if ASTMS is recognized in Mercury, how long will it be before ASTMS and POEU start fighting about the recruitment of telecommunications engineers? Whether the Government will extend a welcome to this form of competition is doubtful.

Union Response After Denationalization

The Logic of Denationalizing

If union power is a characteristic of public ownership, denationalization should roll back that power. What might this actually mean? The nationalized industries, as has been noted, have high union densities often sustained by the closed shop; a preponderance of formal national agreements regulating pay and conditions; and a 'good employer' tradition which stresses 'fairness' in wage setting and the rights of unions to be consulted on corporate plans. There is also evidence that workers in public corporations have led the pack in wage settlements. Logically, therefore, a free marketeer should expect denationalization to bring a more abrasive management attitude to unions, moves against high densities and the closed shop and increased reluctance to consult unions. Also, managements might try to depress wage settlements and fragment national bargaining into plant level bargaining.

Early Days

The honest answer is that it is too early to assess the impact of the first round of sales. And before attempting even a preliminary analysis, several caveats should be entered. It is wrong to see a particular industrial relations tactic (like the decentralization of bargaining) as the preserve of either unions or management, or as necessarily leading to one outcome (like lower wage settlements). Not long ago, devolving bargaining to plant level, with the consequence of 'wage drift', was the pacesetting tactic in the unions (Undy 1978). Even more recently, bargaining decentralization in road haulage, where the NFC is the largest company, was a union tactic. The unions have pushed for a return to plant bargaining in BL which would overturn the centralized bargaining painfully erected by management under Sir Michael Edwardes (*Guardian*, 17 February 1984). Some shop stewards in BS's naval yards have pressed for a return to yard bargaining, which management killed off after nationalization to general acclaim (*Financial Times*, 18 February 1984).

Moreover, still nationalized corporations can display all the characteristics which a free marketeer would expect of the private sector. BSC has decentralized its wage bargaining. BSC, BA and BS have led the economy in shedding jobs and have made zero national pay awards. Since nationalization, manual workers' pay in BS has fallen from 4th to less than 20th in the earnings league. BA has introduced a profit sharing scheme linked to performance. The nationalized airline has also withdrawn facilities from some union representatives, following the management strategy pioneered at the publicly owned BL (*Morning Star*, 15 September 1983).

These examples of managerial toughness might be attributed to the recession and the new political climate. Yet a new study says that 'commercialism' (the attempt to find a set of objectives and criteria which act as market proxies in the nationalized industries) has increasingly formed the context of management's industrial relations strategy in the key area of telecommunications during the past two decades (Batstone, Ferner and Terry 1984). Management's wish to commercialize the telecom business has meant greater flexibility in the use of labour; pay being more closely related to effort; more power for local managers; and more stress on management's right to initiate change, as opposed to the traditional consensual style of industrial relations.

A Preliminary Assessment

In order to make a preliminary assessment of how unions have perceived denationalization, the views of key union officials in the main enterprises so far affected were canvassed. The limitations of this exercise should be stressed. Only one official was interviewed for each enterprise, though in every case that official had substantial bargaining responsibilities. The interviews were conducted by telephone, though a standard set of questions was asked. The officials' responses might be coloured by an awareness of the political implications: they might feel pressure to describe their experiences after denationalization optimistically to demonstrate their competence in defending their members' interests; conversely, they might feel pressure to describe their experiences pessimistically to reinforce their unions' stance against privatization. Also the relatively optimistic responses reported below might change. Denationalization brings with it the uncertainties of the private sector: a striking example is the possible merger of BAe with a company like GEC or Thorn-EMI which was mooted after the interview with the AUEW-TASS official and which must alter radically union perceptions of the BAe denationalization.

Nevertheless, some interesting patterns emerge from the responses received. They are summarized in Table 1 and amplified in the text below. Broadly speaking, the results fit neither what a free marketeer might expect nor the dire forecasts made by unions. According to the respondents, only in AI and C&W have managements attempted to change the bargaining system. This was inevitable in AI, since before denationalization bargaining was done centrally through the UKAEA, of which it was a subsidiary. In C&W, there has been a move to bargain around new profit centres, but Jim Mercer (the divisional officer responsible for C&W in ASTMS, interviewed on 5 March 1984) saw this as an 'opportunity for bargainers' since many C&W staff possess scarce 'high tech' skills. However, management in C&W has had success in amending certain fringe benefits such as expenses.

TABLE 1 How union officials perceive denationalization

	ABP	AI	BAe	Britoil	C&W	NFC
Changes in bargaining system?	No	Yes, better	No	No	Yes	No
Tougher attitude on pay?	No	No, easier	No	No	Mixed	In some respects
Acceleration in job losses?	Yes	No, more jobs	Yes	No, more jobs	Yes	No
Change in consultation?	No	Worse	Better	Better	Yes	No
Change in attitude to unions?	No	Worse	Better	Better	Yes	No
Change in closed shops?	No	Irrelevant	Irrelevant	Irrelevant	Irrelevant	No
Impact of worker shareholders on unions?	None	None	None	None	None	None

Note: This is a very broad summary of the responses received. Refer to the text for amplification.

Views on pay settlements after denationalization followed the same pattern. Chris Darke (national officer for aerospace, AUEW-TASS, interviewed on 14 February 1984) said that the question was academic because settlements in BAe followed the going rate. Freed from public sector constraints, pay has improved considerably in the profitable AI, according to Veronica Bayne, assistant secretary in the CPSA, who was interviewed on 5 March 1984: AI settlements were 7½% in November 1983 and 9½% in November 1982 (Incomes Data Report 1983 a,b). The other respondents reported no change, except that Jack Ashwell, the TGWU's national secretary for commercial vehicles (interviewed on 7 March 1984), complained that the NFC had unilaterally made pay increases before negotiations had been concluded.

Unions in BAe, ABP and C&W are concerned about job losses after denationalization. John Connolly, the TGWU's national docks secretary (interviewed on 5 March 1984), said that recent job losses in ABP — for example, the contracting-out of cleaning staff — stemmed from denationalization. ASTMS added, however, that job losses at C&W were as much due to technological change as to denationalization. Unions in AI and Britoil said that the companies were expanding.

In half the enterprises — BAe, Britoil and C&W — respondents noted changes and in some cases improvements in the way companies consulted unions and in their general attitude to unions. AUEW-TASS said that BAe's need as a private company to lobby for the Government's financial backing for aerospace projects had drawn management and unions together; while nationalized, the employer had seemed 'more remote'. In Britoil, according to Tom Robertson (Glasgow divisional officer, APEX, interviewed on 7 March 1984), unions and management were discussing ways to improve information flows between the two sides. Unions in Britoil were building up membership, unlike 'in the bad old days of BNOC'. In C&W, decisions are taken 'more rapidly', with a 'harder, less personal approach'. This has disadvantages for ASTMS, but also means that decisions are 'less tortuous'. Union facilities at C&W are 'just as good, if not better, than before privatization' but there is less attempt at genuine consultation. In AI there were other complaints. The company, according to the CPSA, has brought in outside staff at director level, consultants and job evaluators who 'have a different attitude. They try to cut corners'.

The closed shop is irrelevant to most enterprises so far denationalized. However there has been no attempt to dismantle the closed shop in ABP. ASTMS said that there was no closed shop in C&W, but the high union membership had stayed firm after flotation.

Finally, all the respondents said that worker shareholders made no difference to industrial relations. This is unsurprising. Unions will clearly ignore workers *qua* shareholders: to do otherwise would undermine their relations to workers *qua* union members. Also, many managements (including the NFC's) have taken a policy decision not to discriminate between worker shareholders and other employees. Unions and management typically do not know if a particular worker is a shareholder. In most denationalized enterprises, the majority of workers became shareholders, not least because shares were given away free. Yet workers typically hold less than 5% of the total shares and worker shareholders lack an independent input into the industrial relations system. The exception is the NFC, where there was a worker buy-out and no free share issue. Only about a half of the NFC workforce are shareholders, but they own more than four fifths of the shares; even here the industrial relations framework has been largely unaffected, though it will be interesting to see whether the decision of the NFC's 1984 AGM to appoint a director who represents the worker shareholders will make any difference.

BR hotels are an exception to the denationalization experiences reported above. Former BR hotels are now held by a number of groups and individuals. Unions are particularly critical of two groups, the Virani brothers who originally bought eight hotels, and the Barclay brothers who own three former BR hotels in London. According to the TSSA, in the Virani hotels workers have been sacked and replaced by others with worse conditions, for example, without travelling concessions or pensions, and have received no pay rises for two years. The TSSA took the Virani brothers to court to get sick pay for one of its members. One new owner has said to the TSSA that BR hotel staff were overpaid by 20%. Both Virani and Barclay are ignoring closed shop agreements and refuse to meet union officials or answer their letters, despite assurances given to the unions before denationalization, according to the TSSA general secretary (BAGWELL, 1984, 47-51).

Unions Changing After Denationalization

There is usually a time lag before unions change their structures to meet changes in the organizations with which they deal. So it is even more premature to assess how denationalization has affected unions. But AI provides some pointers, even though it is unusual in other respects. AI used to be part of the highly centralized civil service bargaining machinery. Negotiations were carried out by the civil service unions' senior officials. With the detachment of AI from this system, bargaining skills — and private sector ones at that — have had to be learned by the next layer down of officials. The sale of the ROFs could give fresh impetus to this diffusion of responsibility within the civil service unions.

The most interesting analysis to date of these sorts of changes is in an NUR paper (NUR 1984). Describing the former BR hotels, it says 'the demands on the union's organization have been transformed'. Before, pay and conditions were dealt with centrally and grievances were referred upwards through the machinery. Now, NUR divisional officers deal with these issues with the separate hotel owners. In consequence, the union is 'conscious of the need to invest more resources' in its weak local organization. With the closed shops in the hotels gone, the NUR has 'to start almost from square one with some of our members re-establishing the benefits of belonging to a trade union. This has had fundamental implications for our recruitment and educational policies'. Much needs to be done, the NUR says, before the union is fully equipped to deal with the new position in the hotels. But, it concludes, 'we recognise that much of this groundwork is a necessary part of progressive trade unionism anyway'.

Conclusion

This concluding comment by the NUR points to what may be one of the most unforeseen consequences of denationalization. If it ends the cosy, centralized management-union understandings which often characterize the public corporations, unions will have to establish a new form of legitimacy among their members. This might entail unions paying greater attention to what their members want and pursuing those wants even more aggressively. As already noted, their recruitment activities too might become more competitive, if liberalization dents the monopolies. These developments would not necessarily entail a weakening of the union movement; possibly the reverse.

This is uncertain, as much that is written about denationalization has to be at present. The major utilities, the core of public enterprise, are so far untouched. Yet three tentative conclusions can be reached. First, unions have in almost all cases failed to stop the sale of public enterprises. A qualification is needed even here, however. Unions may have been exercising negative power in that most early sales have skirted clear of the strongest union bastions. Two economists who have influenced the Government's thinking on privatization have described the NCB as one of the 'prime candidates for privatisation' (Beesley and Littlechild 1983). Yet the Government has taken no steps to sell the NCB or its main subsidiaries, even though, for instance, open cast mining could be sold easily. Second, unions have generally achieved their bargaining objectives before denationalization. Third, unions have in the main protected or even improved their own position and that of their members after denationalization.

The exception to the third conclusion, BR hotels, suggests a fourth, more speculative conclusion. There is no reason to suppose that denationalization will affect workers in different enterprises, and the unions which represent them, in the same way. Some may gain, others will lose. The highly skilled workers in AI improve their wages and numbers; the unskilled workers in the hotels suffer. Highly profitable enterprises have dominated the early sales, so it is unsurprising that their workers and unions have reaped rewards. The fate of the BR hotel workers is so far untypical of the sale of public enterprises, though it is a more familiar outcome in the contracting-out of public services like street cleaning.

Moreover, it is logical to expect the impact of denationalization to vary within enterprises, as well as between enterprises. No large, monopoly-supplier, long established corporation has yet been sold to test this thesis.

But there is evidence for realistic speculation. For example, the MMC found that NCB clerks, tied by internal relativities to miners' pay, were paid 23% above the national average for clerks (MMC 1983, 304). It is unlikely that NCB clerks would retain these external relativities if the NCB were sold and liberalized. The highly skilled operational managers at the pits, on the other hand, might see improvements in their pay and conditions.

Public ownership may have bid up the terms and conditions of less skilled staff (like clerks and some manual workers) with poor bargaining power, and depressed the rewards which highly skilled workers (like managers and engineers) would expect in the private sector. In this precise sense, public ownership has been an egalitarian force. How denationalization will affect the staff of an enterprise will vary, depending not least on what, if any, productivity improvements result and on whether (as is likely) staff experience these productivity increases as fewer jobs, but higher pay. On this, as on many other issues, BT will be the most interesting case yet.

These speculations suggest a final conclusion. Perhaps the unions' greatest success has been to hold a united, anti-privatization line. Denationalization has a variable impact on workers organized by different unions. It could also have a differential impact on workers organized by the same union: the senior grades covered by unions like the EMA might benefit, while the more junior staff lose out. The privatization programme could have split the unions asunder.

5

The Privatization of British Telecommunications

John Kay

Introduction [1]

The lamentable parliamentary debate on the Telecommunications Bill disguised the central issue involved in the privatization of BT. Prior to the Beesley Report (Beesley 1981), most of BT's activities were protected by statutory monopoly. Much of this protection was unnecessary since the technological and economic characteristics of telecommunication systems were such that monopoly was in any case inevitable. This is no longer the case, and as a result there are quite new prospects for the competitive structure of the telecommunications industry in the UK. Does the impending transfer of the ownership of BT to the private sector advance or restrict these competitive opportunities?

The Actors and their Interests

There are several interest groups involved in the process of privatization. Although some nationalized industries still favour the traditional concept of the public corporation, the attitude of BT management to denationalization has generally been supportive. BT is the first of the major state industries to be denationalized, largely as the final resolution of an earlier debate about controls over BT investment. Both the Government and BT have been seeking for some time ways in which BT could raise capital on its own account, free of restrictions imposed by the inclusion of its external finance in the PSBR. Attempts to achieve this by means of a 'Buzby bond' having run into difficulties, the issue is now overtaken, or superseded, by denationalization.

The attractions for BT management of free access to the private capital market are obvious enough. So are the associated reductions in the extent of government scrutiny of its specific investment plans, and of other aspects of its policies. However it is not in the interests of BT management that any reduction in accountability to government should be replaced by an increase in accountability to someone else. Competition provides a degree of accountability to consumers; regulation, to the regulatory authority. If there is substantial debt in the balance sheet, new issues will have to take the form of equity and this would increase the power of shareholders over management. The interests of BT management would therefore be best served by resisting competition and regulation while favouring a low debt/equity ratio on initial flotation. The principal means of securing these interests is to exact concessions from the Government on competition, regulation and the balance sheet in return for management support for denationalization. Competition can also be inhibited by technical measures, such as obstacles to equipment approval and system access; also by predatory pricing, discussed further below.

What are the Government's own objectives in all this? The ideological motivation contains a mixture of strands. There is a belief in the virtues of competition, and in the virtues of private ownership. There is a world-weary anxiety to be rid of the problems of controlling nationalized industries by being rid of the industries themselves. There is a desire for revenue, and an associated anxiety to relieve the anomalies created by the inclusion of public corporation borrowing in the PSBR, not by changes of definition, but by changes in the extent of the public sector. The clearest statement of political objectives is a speech by John Moore (Moore 1983), who signalled a distinct shift in emphasis towards competition and efficiency as the Government's principal objectives.

The principal union involved in BT is the POEU which, like the other unions affected, has opposed privatization. Any reduction in political influence on telecommunications development is likely to be accompanied by a reduction in union influence on telecommunications development, and indeed this seems to be a thinly-disguised Government objective. The POEU is also in the front line of concerted general union opposition to privatization — it may, in a sense, be seen as a stalking horse for cases elsewhere in the public sector where the damage both to unions and to the interests of their members is much more clearly evident than is the case in telecommunications.

The POEU has three principal methods of deploying its opposition — political influence, industrial action and publicity. Its feeling of impotence in relation to the first of these routes is clearly indicated by the fact that the main tactic of its sponsored MP, John Golding, in leading the parliamentary opposition was the use of the filibuster. Industrial action, mainly aimed against Mercury, the projected competitive telecommunications network, fell away in the face of legal attack and limited membership support. An advertising campaign, largely centred on ridiculous allegations about dangers to national security and the possibility of charges for emergency calls, provoked some counter-advertising by BT itself.

The interests of telecommunications workers themselves are less easy to discern. On the one hand, if denationalization does lead to increased efficiency by BT the main scope for cost reduction is in lower staffing levels; on the other, if investment is greater then employment opportunities may by increased (although newer technology is itself likely to be labour saving). On wages, two diametrically opposite views of the present situation are possible. One is that BT employees currently share some of the rents accruing to a telecommunications monopoly, and hence that moves to reduce that monopoly, or to share its spoils with private investors, would lead to lower wage levels all round. The other is that BT as a monopoly buyer of the services of telecommunications workers uses that power to depress wages below levels which would be formed in a competitive market, and hence competition would be likely to lead to higher earnings. Probably each view has some relevance for particular groups of employees. The one group for whom the direction of changes is relatively unambiguous is senior management; most instances of denationalization already accomplished have been followed, if not accompanied, by upward movements of salary levels towards market rates.

Suppliers of telecommunications equipment also have a stake in the outcome. There are three principal suppliers in the UK — the General Electric Company, Plessey and Standard Telephones and Cables — and their interest is principally in ensuring that privatization does lead to an increase in overall investment in telecommunications and does not lead to an increase in competition for the resulting orders, either from imports or from manufacturing activities by BT itself. This cause is partly conducted by discreet lobbying. GEC has shown particular political skills of this kind, having increasingly concentrated its activities in areas in which demand is determined politically rather than in the market place. It has also been maintained more publicly in the House of Lords, where Lord Weinstock has led opposition to provisions of the Telecommunications Bill with support from other peers who share with him not only the benches of the House of Lords but the seats of the boardroom of GEC.

Consumer interests might appear to lie principally in the provision of a cheap and efficient telecommunications network. However, the reality is more complex. Behind the framework of statutory monopoly, extensive patterns of cross-subsidization have emerged and consumers who currently benefit from this have sought to defend the interests concerned. These include the provision of uneconomic services such as emergency and rural services. The maintenance of such services has never seriously been in question. They are sustained in the US by private telephone companies, partly for public relations reasons and partly because of a perception that the long run interest of promoting universal telephone service and use far outweighs the short run costs involved, just as petrol wholesalers have continued to service hopelessly uneconomic outlets in rural areas (MMC 1979). However, at least until the later stages of the argument, BT has not been active in discouraging fears about the future of such provisions, perhaps because it has been accepted that the burden of providing such services will influence the level of access charges which BT may make to potential competitors. In consequence the issue has absorbed a wholly disproportionate quantity of backbenchers' mail and parliamentary time.

The existing tariff structure is one in which local networks are subsidized from trunk and international calls, which has the incidental effect of favouring residential customers at the expense of business users. There is, of course, no such thing as a cross-subsidy from business to persons, since all costs fall on consumers in one way or another in the end. But this link is not always immediately transparent. The issue of tariff rebalancing — in which measures to promote a more competitive environment lead to a shift in the cost of telephone services from business to persons — has become a major political issue in the US and simmers below the surface in the UK. It is discussed further below.

The final actor is Mercury, the consortium established by BP, C&W and Barclays Merchant Bank to provide a range of telecommunications services in competition with BT. Mercury's performance has so far been disappointing and the first Mercury call is still to be made. Barclays Merchant Bank has sought to extricate itself but no new UK backer of similar substance has yet been found. Pacific Telesis — the West Coast arm of the newly disintegrated US Bell System — has emerged as a somewhat unwelcome suitor, but one which may be presumed to have a greater relevant management capability than any of the existing participants.

The Development of Competition

Competitive opportunities in telecommunications have been greatly increased by technological change in the industry. The issue of liberalization may now arise in any of four major areas of telecommunications services: terminal equipment, local network, call connection and value added services.

It is difficult to see that there were ever arguments for restricting competition in terminal equipment stronger than the arguments for giving the electricity industry a monopoly of the appliances which might be plugged into its network, and indeed since unsatisfactory electrical appliances are, unlike unsatisfactory telephones, hazardous to life, the case for restriction is probably a good deal stronger in electricity. The consequences of liberalization for the range and cost of equipment available to consumers are already apparent in high street shops. Competition has not yet developed fully; in the initial stages BT was dilatory in approving equipment while the new British Approvals Board for Telecommunications displays classic capture symptoms. It is not immediately obvious why, for example, it is necessary to visit the factory in which an item of equipment is made in order to assess its suitability for attachment to the British telephone network.

The establishment of local telephone networks is an obvious natural monopoly. It is likely that technological developments will alter this in due course. The most likely source of such change in the short term would be the provision of 'voice-over' services in cable networks developed for other purposes. Under the present cabling proposals (Industry and Trade Committee 1982), these facilities can only be provided through BT or Mercury and BT is itself a participant in a number of prospective cable consortia.

Call connection was also traditionally a natural monopoly, but technical changes have both reduced costs and ensured that scale economies are exhausted at relatively low levels of traffic. The combination of these two factors means that competition in these areas is now possible and likely to be profitable because tariffs have not been reduced in line with the fall in costs, with the revenue being used to cross-subsidize less profitable services. Such competition can be provided either by the installation of separate facilities or by the resale of capacity leased from BT. Both methods are used by the alternative long distance networks which exist in the US. Such competition as is to be permitted in the UK will come from Mercury, and by the first of these methods. To be of substantial use, it is necessary that access to the BT network should be available so that a Mercury facility can be used for part, but not necessarily the whole, of a call. The cost and terms of such access are issues of some importance. After extended dispute, the basis of access has now been settled on terms reasonably favourable to Mercury. This also matters in relation to competition in the provision of value added services — the use of the telephone network as a basis for more sophisticated services.

Ownership Transfer Versus Competition

Two alternative political objectives — liberalization and denationalization — have been defined above. The former will inevitably be resisted by management; the latter, on appropriate terms, will be welcomed. Thus in securing political support for denationalization from management, the trading off of concessions on liberalization — or its absence — for support of the strategy of changing ownership has inevitably seemed an attractive one. In any event, the liberalization battle is a peculiarly difficult one for politicians to fight. It is hard to distinguish the genuine technical objection from the spurious, and effective rights of access or interconnection depend not only on a decision of principle but also on what happens at many different points of the BT network.

There is another area in which the objectives of liberalization and denationalization necessarily conflict. The greater the degree of competition to which BT is subject, the less, at any given level of efficiency, will be its profits; and so the lower its share price. The caveat is an important one. It is conceivable that competition could have a beneficial effect on efficiency which would increase profits by more than the erosion of monopoly power would reduce them, and the threat (rather than the actuality) of competition might well have such an effect. However, even if more competition would on balance be likely to increase rather than reduce profitability, the greater uncertainty of a more competitive environment could only reduce share values. This point acquires considerably more significance after denationalization than before. It is possible for a government to argue that it is more concerned with consumer benefits than with revenue and share prices. It is not possible for private shareholders to take a similarly altruistic line. It therefore follows that an effect of denationalization is to establish a new, and widely spread lobby against further liberalization or new competition.

If competition is likely to be limited in the foreseeable future, some degree of regulation is required. This is to be accomplished through OFTEL, a body loosely modelled on the Office of Fair Trading. OFTEL has a Director-General — Bryan Carsberg, Professor of Accounting at the London School of Economics — and its own professional staff. Its formal relations with BT are governed by the terms of BT's licence (Department of Industry 1984). The enforcement of the conditions of the licence falls to OFTEL, modifications to it to the MMC.

The role which OFTEL will in fact play is yet to be determined. An obvious danger is that it will be the subject of regulatory capture so that, dependent on BT for information and expertise, it comes to equate the interests of BT with the needs of an efficient telecommunications system. A subsidiary danger, but one with a similar outcome in practice, is that it becomes a consumerist pressure group, reacting to the levels of complaints by individual customers about the quality of their telephone service that formerly went to MPs: a souped-up Post Office Users' National Council, equally little match for the interests of producer pressure groups.

The most valuable protection for consumers is competition rather than the activities of representative bodies, and the real test of OFTEL will be the degree of success it enjoys in promoting and protecting such competition. An important difference between the US, with its extensive experience of regulation of privately owned monopolies, and the UK is that there is no British equivalent of its anti-predation legislation. Although the American courts have encountered considerable difficulty in achieving effective definitions of predation, the opportunities for private enforcement through the courts and exemplary treble damages in demonstrated cases have important deterrent effects. The remedies available to a British company in telecommunications which feels itself the victim of predatory activity by BT is that of appeal to OFTEL, which can then, if persuaded of the validity of the complaint, tell BT to stop. Although substantial improvements to BT's internal accounting procedures are in train, it would in many cases be difficult for an insider, more so an outsider, to tell whether proposed prices were related to costs or not. The experience of NBC in successfully fighting off competition on many of its routes since liberalization in 1980 is instructive.

Its National Express subsidiary was vigorous in responding to competitive fares. It is open to argument whether the resulting fares structure was predatory, but clear that the question of whether or not it was predatory was not an important one for those responsible. No prospective entrant to telecommunications could derive confidence from this experience.

OFTEL will also be responsible for monitoring the implementation of the tariff regulation formula. Following the Littlechild Report (Littlechild 1983), the Government agreed that BT should be required to limit annual tariff increases to 3% less than the rate of inflation — the so-called (RPI-x) formula. The objective is to restrict profits while leaving BT with an incentive to increased efficiency. The formula contrasts with the common US scheme, based on rates of return on costs, which gives no encouragement to keep these costs to the lowest possible level.

There are two major problems which an (RPI-x) formula must confront. What is the basket of services to which it should be applied? And what should be the choice of 'x', the gap between the inflation rate and the rate of rise in price of the telecommunications service? Littlechild's intention was that price restriction should be confined to services not subject to competition, and that it should be limited to the period needed for competition to become effective, which he optimistically suggested might be five years. The basket of services chosen is, in the event, a comparatively broad one, embracing the major BT services except for international calls and some other services which are clearly the subject of effective competition.

The basis on which 'x' should be chosen is a matter of some difficulty. It is reasonable for x to be positive, as there is scope for considerable productivity gains in telecommunications, most dramatically in the short term as a result of the introduction of digital switching. But if x were to be based on BT costs, then the formula is equivalent for all practical purposes to rate of return regulation. In principle, x should be based not on what is happening to BT cost levels, but on what *ought* to be happening to BT costs; but there is no evident source of such information. Foreign experience may provide some guide.

Both competition and tariff regulation raise the issue of 'tariff rebalancing'. Recent productivity improvements have lowered the real cost of long distance calls much more rapidly than the cost of local calls and basic telephone service provision. However, tariffs have only partly reflected this change, and the differential between long and short distance calls still reflects past rather than present relative costs. The profitability of international services is particularly great. The ways in which prices diverge from costs is by no means straightforward; for example, the London local calling area, which covers around 20% of the whole BT network, contains many more subscribers than can sensibly be defended on cost grounds.

Most of this elaborate pattern of cross-subsidization is arbitrary, historical in origin, and reflects inertia or administrative convenience rather than conscious choices. But a more profit-oriented organization is likely to want to expand over-priced services, and contract loss-making ones; and even if it is not so inclined, competitive pressures, which will tend to concentrate on profitable areas of the business, will force it to do so. The result will be a rebalancing of tariffs which, in the main, will favour business as against residential subscribers.

Problems of Flotation

The flotation of a 51% stake in BT would be by far the largest equity capital raising exercise ever undertaken in the UK. The £2-4bn. which such a sale might produce may be compared with the largest issue so far, a £600m. rights issue by BP. The size of the issue is itself something of a problem, but one which should not be exaggerated. The amounts involved are not out of proportion to the net cash flows of investing institutions, and, while a sudden call for this amount would pose considerable difficulties for markets, the issue has been anticipated for some time and is likely to be accompanied by facilities for staged payment.

The amounts to be raised depend on a number of factors, of which the most important are the market rating attached to BT shares and the capital structure with which it is endowed on flotation. BT has some of the characteristics of a regulated utility, such as US power or telephone companies, which in the main command dull stock market ratings; and some of the characteristics of an electrical stock, which the market views much more favourably. Perhaps the most closely comparable security is C&W, itself the subject of recent flotation, which operates in various fields of telecommunications overseas, particularly in Hong Kong, and which is a partner in Mercury. In practice the stock market has very little idea of how to value BT; the difficulties of regulation are very real; the purchase is essentially a political assessment of the amount of money which BT will be allowed, or will wish to make in a regulatory and competitive environment of unpredictable intensity and uncertain duration.

The amount to be raised will also depend on the extent to which BT debt to the Government is turned into equity on flotation. The greater the amount of debt in the balance sheet, the lower will be the Government's immediate receipts from sale, and the larger its future income. The less debt BT has before flotation, the more debt it can incur after flotation without facing difficulties from the capital market. It follows that both the Government and BT have an interest in promoting an initial balance sheet with comparatively little debt. One item which is likely to remain in the balance sheet is a 'debt' acquired as a result of the complex pension funding arrangements which were introduced when the Post Office became a public corporation in 1969.

Conclusion

It is difficult to see the transfer of 51% of the equity of BT into private hands as a sensible objective in its own right. The reason for promoting it is because it is thought it will, directly or indirectly, make BT more efficient; or because it will increase BT's investment freedom; or because it will raise revenue; or any other of the multiple objectives which governments pursue in their dealings with both private and nationalized industries. But it seems that the politics of privatization have made it an objective in its own right and, successively, the possibilities of restructuring the organization, of introducing effective competition, and finally of raising substantial revenue, have all been relegated to a minor place in pursuit of the political imperative of denationalization. The BT flotation will be deemed a success if it is completed without any of the accidents which appear to have dogged the mechanics of flotation so far. The political achievement of having got so far in the face of endless Whitehall warnings of the difficulties in the way and the unsuitability of the time is certainly a considerable one; but the promotion of an efficient telecommunications system has had to take something of a backseat in consequence.

This objective is rather poorly represented by any of the major interest groups described in this chapter. It is probably best served by promoting competition as rapidly as possible, but no individual agent has this as a goal. Even Mercury has concern only for a limited form of competition that restricts entry after the number of participants gets to two. The hope of competition nevertheless rests with Mercury and OFTEL: the two newest, and as yet weakest, participants in the game. Rapid denationalization is actually an obstacle to the promotion of liberalization.

The prospect of flotation introduces a new group of agents — the shareholders of BT. The hope — and indeed the rationale of denationalization — is that their interest will be in securing greater profits through greater efficiency within BT. The difficulty to be confronted is that the same objective can equally well, and perhaps more easily, be achieved by resisting both competition and regulation. And in this they are likely to have the support of BT itself.

NOTE

1 The author wishes to acknowledge the financial support of the ESRC for the work from which this article derives.

6

Privatization of the Electricity and Gas Industries

Michael Webb

Introduction

The UK Government is in the process of implementing an ambitious programme of privatization, both in the sense of transferring assets from the public to the private sector (denationalization) and with the removal of statutory barriers to competition (liberalization). Energy industries have figured prominently in this programme. Thus the production activities of BNOC have been denationalized as Britoil and the oil interests of BGC are in the process of being shifted to the private sector.

Although the Government has not published a programme for the privatization of the remaining public sector energy industries, it has made it clear that they are all likely to be affected. The reasons for privatization were discussed in a speech given by the Financial Secretary to the Treasury last November (Moore 1983). Most of these reasons were said to apply to all nationalized industries and were not industry specific. The Financial Secretary noted that in the past it was often claimed that for a number of industries the public interest was best served by having a monopoly supplier since competition would in some sense be wasteful. He, however, argued that there are very few natural monopolies[1] and that 'electricity generation, the production and marketing of gas, coal production and sale,...are in no sense natural monopolies' (Moore 1983, 3). In consequence, he said, it is by no means self-evident that monopolies in these areas are either necessary or beneficial.

The principal objectives of the privatization programme appear to be the promotion of a more efficient allocation of resources by encouraging competition and reducing costs, and making the industries more responsive to consumers' wants. Mr Moore claimed that the performance of nationalized industries has been disappointing when assessed by 'any criteria'. 'Public enterprises perform relatively poorly in terms of their competitive position, use labour and capital inefficiently, and are less profitable' (Moore 1983, 5). It should be noted, however, that for a number of reasons it is very difficult to assess the performance of nationalized industries. Two reasons are, first, that nationalized industries are expected to pursue multiple, and sometimes conflicting, objectives, and second, that these industries are subject to political interference in their day-to-day operations. There is a lack of good empirical evidence comparing the relative efficiency of comparable private and public sector firms in the UK. Millward (1982) has surveyed evidence from other countries for electricity supply and some other industries. His conclusion was that available evidence did not support the general contention that public sector firms are less efficient than comparable private sector firms.

The argument that privatization will encourage competition is clearly dependent on the form in which industries are privatized. When privatization leaves the number of competing firms unchanged and simply involves the substitution of a private sector firm for a public sector firm (as happened with BNOC's production activities) then it is difficult to see why competition will necessarily be increased. The various arguments for the privatization of energy industries have been considered by Webb (1984a).

The principal purpose of this chapter is to analyze the possible denationalization of those activities of the electricity and gas industries which have been identified as likely candidates by Mr Moore. No attention is given to the coal industry since the Secretary of State for Energy (Mr Peter Walker) has recently made it clear that the Government is not seriously considering privatization of this industry (*Hansard*, 20 February 1984, col. 550). The chapter begins, however, by reviewing briefly the history of privatization in the energy sector.

History of Privatization in the Energy Sector

To date, the policy of denationalization has affected BGC and BNOC, while liberalization has affected BGC and the electricity supply industry. Denationalization has been concerned with BNOC's oil producing business and with BGC's onshore and offshore oil assets and gas showrooms. Liberalization has involved the removal of the prohibition on any organization other than an electricity board supplying electricity as its main business activity, and has required BGC, if requested, to operate its pipeline system as a common carrier.

So far the most important Act relating to the energy industries is the Oil and Gas (Enterprise) Act 1982. This Act made provision for the denationalization of the offshore oil assets of both BGC and BNOC. The latter was established on 1 January 1976 under the terms of the Petroleum and Submarine Pipe-lines Act 1975, as a dual function enterprise. On the one hand it was to search for and produce oil (its production activity), and on the other to trade in oil (through its participation rights in North Sea oil fields).[2] The Oil and Gas (Enterprise) Act authorized the sale of BNOC's oil and gas production interests but left untouched its trading interests. In early 1982, BNOC was responsible for 7% of North Sea oil production through its interests in nine North Sea oil fields and one gas field. Its trading activities, which have a number of objectives including ensuring oil supplies in times of national emergency and exercising some control over North Sea oil prices through the operation of participation agreements, both remain and are expected to remain in the public sector.

The denationalization of BNOC's production activities occurred as follows. On 4 March 1982, a new company, Britoil, was registered in Scotland but did not undertake any business in the period 4 March to 31 July. The Secretary of State for Energy, using powers given under the terms of the Oil and Gas (Enterprise) Act 1982, directed BNOC to transfer its oil and gas production and exploration business to Britoil. The Secretary of State approved such a scheme on 28 July and it came into force on 1 August 1982, when Britoil commenced trading as a wholly owned subsidiary of BNOC. Britoil's share capital was transferred to the Secretary of State and his nominee on 1 November. On 4 November, Britoil was re-registered as a public company and subsequently, on 19 November, the Secretary of State offered for sale up to 255.2m. ordinary shares (51% of the total), at a minimum tender price of 215p per share. However, only 69.8m. shares were sold so that the underwriters had to take up the remaining 185.4m., thus ensuring that the sale realized the expected £549m.

The Oil and Gas (Enterprise) Act 1982 also allowed for the denationalization of BGC's offshore oil assets. Two sets of directions have been issued under the terms of that Act. The first was issued in August 1982 and covered BGC's interests in six oil fields (Beryl A, Beryl B, Montrose, Hutton, North West Hutton and Fulmar), of which only two (Beryl A and Montrose) were operating. It was required to draw up a scheme for the transfer of its interests in these fields to four new subsidiaries owned by a new holding company. Following the drawing-up of this scheme, the fields were transferred to British Gas North Sea Holdings Ltd. on 1 May 1983. The first set of directions also required BGC to establish participation arrangements in advance of disposal of its interests in the six fields. These arrangements were concerned with options to acquire up to 51% of oil and gas liquids produced in the fields. BGC was directed to establish participation arrangements between itself and the new subsidiary companies, and to then transfer these rights to a new company which the Government would subsequently transfer to BNOC. The BGC conformed with this requirement by transferring its participation rights to British Gas Petroleum Acquisition and Development Ltd. (British Gas PAD Ltd.) on 2 May 1983.

The second set of directions concerning BGC's offshore oil interests was issued in July 1983. These required BGC to draw up a scheme to transfer its interests in eight offshore licences to a new subsidiary and to establish participation arrangements which would subsequently be transferred to BNOC. BGC was later required to transfer both British Gas North Sea

Holdings Ltd. and British Gas PAD Ltd. to the Secretary of State for Energy. This transfer became effective on 1 September 1983, and British Gas North Sea Holdings Ltd. was renamed Enterprise Oil. The Government has appointed a part-time chairman for Enterprise Oil and announced that it intends to sell all of its ordinary shares through a stock market flotation. The flotation is expected to occur in 1984-85 and to raise about £400m.

In October 1981, acting under powers contained in section 7.2 of the Gas Act 1972, the Secretary of State for Energy required BGC to dispose of its 50% production and licensing interests in Dorset, including the Wytch Farm oil field which it owned on a 50:50 basis with BP. These onshore oil assets of BGC were not considered to be sufficiently attractive to float off on the Stock Exchange and it was decided that they should be offered by tender to existing oil companies. The highest bid was made by the Dorset Group (led by Tricentrol) in 1982. This bid, however, was substantially lower than BGC's valuation of its Wytch Farm assets, and protracted negotiations followed between the two parties. In 1983, BGC was valuing its share of Wytch Farm at about £350m; while an independent valuation assessed it at £250m. The successful Dorset Group bid was for only £160m., payable in two equal instalments, plus a share of the profits in the later stages of the field's life.[3]

The Government has also been concerned with the denationalization of BGC's gas showrooms. In July 1981, following a report of the Monopolies and Mergers Commission (1980), the Government announced that BGC should withdraw from retailing and dispose of its showrooms. Their disposal has, in fact, been delayed, partly because of fears about possible effects on safety standards regarding the installation and maintenance of gas appliances. It should be noted, however, that at May 1984 the Government's announcement regarding the denationalization of gas showrooms still stands.

Policy on liberalization has so far affected BGC and the electricity supply industry. The Oil and Gas (Enterprise) Act 1982 removed BGC's right to buy 51% of all North Sea gas and required it, if requested, to run its pipeline system as a common carrier. Similarly, the Energy Act 1983 removed the restriction on private owners of power stations using the public transmission and distribution system to transmit their electricity. It also removed the prohibition on any organization other than an electricity board supplying electricity as its main business activity.

The foregoing represent the privatization measures which have occurred to date in the energy sector. It will be observed that there is no uniformity in the denationalization measures. In two cases (Enterprise Oil and Wytch Farm), denationalization involves 100% sale to the private sector. In the case of Britoil, however, the Government has retained a 49% shareholding. Thus, the problems discussed later in this book by David Steel are relevant to Britoil. It is worth noting that the Government has not been very adventurous in its choice of denationalization methods: it has not used franchising of assets in an attempt to stimulate competition, for example.

Yet, if the Government's policy is going to be successful, it must stimulate competition (Kay and Silberston 1984).

Denationalization of Electricity Supply

The possible denationalization of electricity generation, that is the sale of power stations, is considered in this section. Following Mr Moore, it will be assumed that the transmission grid does have natural monopoly characteristics and thus will be operated by a public sector firm. The emphasis of this section is on the various economic and technical characteristics of the electricity supply industry (ESI) which are crucial to discussion of possible denationalization.

At the present time, the ESI in England and Wales is vertically integrated and consists of 12 area boards, which are responsible for the distribution and sale of electricity, the CEGB, which is responsible for the generation[4] and transmission of electricity plus its sale to the area boards, and the Electricity Council, which is a forum where the general policy of the supply industry is discussed. Although the CEGB and area boards must consult the Electricity Council on tariffs, investment programmes and some other matters, the Council has no powers to direct or control the boards. In Scotland and Northern Ireland, electricity supply is the responsibility of boards which are independent of those in England and Wales. For ease of exposition, attention will be confined to possible denationalization of the ESI in England and Wales.

The CEGB views itself as engaging in two main activities as prescribed by the Electricity Acts of 1947 and 1957:

(i) the planning, development and construction of an integrated system of power stations, transmission lines and sub-stations to meet forecast demand at an acceptable quality of supply at least cost; and

(ii) the operation of that system in all periods in a secure and efficient manner to meet demand in all periods at least cost.

Although the CEGB has recently been criticized (Monopolies and Mergers Commission 1981b) with regard to certain aspects of its investment appraisal methods and their application (criticisms which have led to reforms), there is little doubt that in general it employs sophisticated methods of investment appraisal and system control. Considering activity (ii) above, it seeks to minimize the fuel costs of meeting the demand for electricity by ranking its generating sets in a 'merit order' of variable operating costs (basically fuel costs) and follows increases and decreases in demand by loading or off-loading generating sets in order of merit. Thus, higher fuel cost sets are only used once lower fuel cost sets have been loaded. In this connection, the CEGB has established seven regional grid control centres, each of which is responsible for the operation of the grid in its area. These centres are, however, responsible to and controlled by the national control centre in London which is concerned with the efficient and secure operation of the integrated national grid via the merit order operation of all generating sets (allowing for transmission losses and a few other factors which interfere with the pure merit order working of the supply system).

The CEGB's investment appraisal methods are concerned with meeting forecast demand for electricity at least cost. New generating projects are selected using DCF techniques with a system planning model which simulates the operation of generation and transmission plants over a planning period, using assumptions with regard to future electricity demand, fuel costs, capital costs of different types of plant, etc. In this way, the CEGB attempts to identify and then construct an optimal plant mix, that is a mix of power plants with different cost characteristics to meet forecast demand at least cost. Thus, it tends to construct plants with relatively high capital costs but low running costs to meet long duration (base) loads, and plants with relatively low capital costs but high running costs to meet short duration (peak) loads. At the present time, the CEGB has excess capacity, a situation which is expected to continue to the end of this century.

In the context of this planning system, it is important to consider the denationalization of generation from two points of view: the sale of existing power stations; and the construction of new power stations financed by private investors. Since the latter may be anticipated to lead to an important set of problems which may affect the optimal (least cost) development of the power system, this aspect will be considered first.

Generation projects have a number of features which will be assessed by potential investors. These include the fact that power stations are relatively expensive. For example, in terms of 1984 prices, a 1,000 MW coal-fired power station would cost in the region of £800m., and a similar size nuclear station in the region of £1150m. These projects are not only expensive but typically have long lead times (including construction periods) and long operating lives. Thus, a large coal-fired station may take 7 or 8 years to construct and then operate for 40 years. The combination of these features means that, in discounted terms, these projects generally have very long (in excess of 20 years) payback periods. As would be anticipated, given these features, investment in individual power stations operated in integrated supply systems is subject to considerable risk and uncertainty. For example, the forecast rate of return to power stations could be reduced if demand is less than was forecast or if costs rise due to the imposition of environmental standards.

In these circumstances, investment in new power stations may not appear to be relatively attractive to private investors, especially if prices are regulated (see below). Another feature which would operate in this way is that, whether private investors own one or a small number of power stations, they must give control over the use made of those stations to the organization responsible for the operation of the national grid system. This is a basic requirement for meeting the national demand for electricity at least cost with plants operated in merit order. This giving over of control applies equally to existing individual power stations which are denationalized and to new stations which are constructed in the future.

From an investment planning point of view, a similar point relates to the loss of control by private investors over the generating stations which should be constructed if the optimal plant mix is to be established and forecast demand for electricity met at least cost. As has been seen, the selection of generation projects is (and should be) made on a total system basis. Presumably, if generating projects were denationalized but the integrated transmission system was owned and operated as a public sector utility, there would need to be a separate, but central, organization responsible for (among other things) investment planning. Unlike the Electricity Council, this new organization would need effective powers of direction and control, for otherwise it would not be possible to ensure that least cost projects were selected. Thus, the situation might be one where this new organization identified preferred projects which private investors were then invited to finance. When compared with potential investments in other parts of the economy, this investment in new power stations may not appear very attractive, especially if rates of return are regulated.

The previously mentioned difficulties would be most acute if denationalization occurred on a piecemeal basis with all power stations having different owners. Problems of investment decision-making would be reduced, the fewer the number of owners of power stations. Thus the more the market structure with regard to generation approximates to perfect competition, the greater are likely to be the problems of constructing optimal plant mixes and meeting forecast electricity demand at least cost.

A number of the foregoing difficulties will be less acute when considering the denationalization of existing power stations. But some of them, including the giving up of control as required for the merit order operation of plants, will remain. When considered in aggregate, these problems raise the question of whether the ESI will continue to be operated as a single entity in conformity with the least cost objective, or will be operated as a set of interdependent supply boards, each with its own objectives, and the interconnections between them being used to provide security of supply in unfavourable circumstances. If the latter were to happen, then denationalization would probably be required on a supply board basis (but possibly with much smaller boards than the existing 12 area boards), with the concomitant requirement for groups of investors to find very large sums indeed.[5] The planning and operation of the supply system on a disjointed basis would probably lead to an increase in the costs of meeting forecast demand. Any increased costs should be offset against efficiency and other gains which protagonists of denationalization of electricity supply anticipate will result from that action. This, of course, is a general point and relates to all the increased costs which might result from denationalization, including those associated with establishing and operating an appropriate regulatory system (with its associated compliance costs).

It is clearly important to enquire about the potential benefits which might be expected to accrue from the denationalization of existing power stations. In this situation, the plant mix and technical characteristics of the set of power stations will be given, and will continue to be given for many years. At the present time, 58% of the CEGB's costs which are reflected in its Bulk Supply Tariff (BST) relate to fuel costs.Since the efficiency with which stations can convert different fuels into electricity will be inherited (though this can be influenced by management), the main potential for lower costs must come from lower fuel input prices. If the main supplier of power station coal continues to be the NCB, why should fuel input prices fall? In fact the reverse could occur, since with many owners of power stations, the CEGB's existing techniques, designed to minimize electricity production costs, might be abandoned.[6] The optimal allocation of fuel on a total system basis may be replaced by sub-optimization on an area basis. There are, however, two potential ways in which fuel input costs may be reduced (on a financial basis, but not necessarily on an economic basis). One concerns the use of coal imports, and raises the question of whether denationalization of generating stations would be likely to be accompanied by a major policy change regarding coal imports. The other concerns the possibility that private companies may be able to negotiate lower prices with the NCB.

The optimal generating capacity of an electric power utility will be a function of many variables, including the forecast demand for electricity and the quality (reliability) of service to be offered to consumers. Total capacity will be planned to exceed forecast maximum demand, to allow for planned and unplanned plant unavailability, and uncertainty with regard to the load forecast. If denationalization of generating stations was to occur on a station by station basis, then the provision of excess capacity required for the security of supply objective might pose a number of problems. For example, the transmission utility might need to enter into security contracts concerned with specifying reliability of supply, independent of direct purchases of power.

The denationalization of some or all generating stations will have implications for the setting of electricity tariffs, including the CEGB's BST, which is the tariff used for sales to the 12 area boards. Following the limited liberalization measures which were introduced in the 1983 Energy Act, the area boards have had to publish several new tariffs. These cover (i) the terms on which the boards will purchase electricity generated by a private generator; (ii) the terms on which private generators or suppliers are permitted to use a board's supply system for the purpose of providing a supply to any premises; and (iii) the terms on which a board will supply premises supplied by a private generator or supplier, including the place of private generation. Tariffs for (i) and (iii) are related to the BST. The denationalization of generating capacity would require the development of a new tariff (which would affect the BST) to define the terms on which the transmission utility would purchase electricity. If the overall objective is to remain that of meeting demand for electricity at least cost, and thus the supply system is to be treated as a single entity (irrespective of the actual ownership of different segments), then the new tariff needs to be established on a marginal cost basis. In addition, this tariff must be consistent with the merit order operation of generating sets.

Looking ahead to the situation where the generating stations have been denationalized, it is important to consider potential problems concerned with agreeing new rates and/or structures for this tariff. The situation is likely to be one where a monopsonist (the transmission utility) faces either a single seller (all generating stations sold to a private sector monopolist) or a variable number of sellers with a limit number equal to the number of power stations. The larger the number of parties with which the transmission utility has to negotiate, the more costly and difficult is likely to be the determination of an agreed tariff.

Finally, considering this tariff, it is important to note that if the organization of the industry is private generation with public sector transmission and distribution, then there will remain a requirement for a civil service involvement at a similar level to the existing one. If a regulatory body is established, then there could conceivably be an increase in the number of civil servants or analogous persons involved with the general external supervision of the ESI.

Problems of regulation for the ESI are likely to be similar to those of regulating the gas industry. Discussion of issues relating to regulation is deferred to a later section.

Denationalization of Gas

At the present time, the gas supply industry is vertically integrated with BGC being concerned with the exploration/production of natural gas, its transmission through an integrated system, and its marketing. The Government appears to accept that the transmission of gas is subject to economies of scale and is to be viewed as a natural monopoly (Moore 1983). Thus, the denationalization of gas is likely to concern, on the one hand, the sale of gas fields and production facilities, and, on the other hand, the transfer of gas marketing operations to the private sector. It should, however, be noted that the present chairman of BGC has stated that in his view if BGC is to be denationalized then it should be kept as a single entity. Such a change would, of course, mean replacing a public sector monopoly with a private sector monopoly.

At various times, BGC has set up five wholly owned subsidiaries concerned with the exploration and production of hydrocarbons offshore and onshore. The original subsidiary was Gas Council (Exploration) Limited which currently has interests in various consortia concerned with the exploration, development and production of natural gas. Previously, it also had oil interests, which were the subject of denationalization at Wytch Farm and as Enterprise Oil. Technically, and unlike the denationalization of power stations, the sale of these gas fields should pose few problems. But their denationalization will raise a number of important questions concerning equity and optimal resource allocation. One dimension of the equity issue concerns the likely market valuation of these fields. For a number of reasons, including different attitudes to risk and the use of different (higher) discount rates, it is likely that the market value will be lower than that given by BGC.[7] There is thus likely to be a redistribution of income away from citizens and taxpayers (the present 'owners' of BGC) towards the new owners of the gas fields.[8]

The most interesting and difficult problems are likely to be posed by the denationalization of gas marketing operations. One of these will concern the determination of gas tariffs and the possible involvement of a regulatory commission. Likely problems associated with this are discussed in the next section. A very basic problem will involve the determination of the boundary between gas transmission and distribution and hence the scope of the marketing units to be denationalized. Similarly, the appropriate size of those units, and thus their geographical coverage, must be determined. If these units are made too small in order to make them attractive to investors, there may be an increase in costs compared with those of BGC (such as for administration, meter reading, billing, etc.). This point is potentially very important, since it is claimed that denationalization will lead to more cost efficiency.

As with electricity supply, a careful case needs to be made out detailing the benefits which are expected to accrue from denationalization of gas supply, since otherwise the case rests on political dogma and arbitrary decisions concerning which industries are included in the public sector. An interesting exercise would be to consider the potential impact of denationalization on the recommendations made by Deloitte, Haskins & Sells (1983) in their efficiency study of BGC. There is insufficient space here to undertake this exercise. However, it is worth noting that the Deloittes' report was very critical of BGC's failure to relate gas prices to LRMC. To say the least, it is not at all clear that denationalization of gas marketing would lead to gas tariffs being more closely related to marginal costs. In fact, denationalization with regulation might be antagonistic to this pricing policy (see the next section).

Before leaving this brief discussion, it should be noted that denationalization of BGC's marketing activities is likely to occur after the sale of its gas showrooms and will probably encounter many of the objections which have delayed that. In particular, concern will be expressed about possible effects on the safety of gas appliances, gas distribution systems, maintenance standards, etc. These concerns will probably mean that denationalization will be accompanied by regulation of gas safety standards.

Some Issues of Regulation

Denationalization of the electricity supply and gas industries (or parts of them) is likely to be accompanied by the introduction of some system of regulation. For example, denationalization of the marketing of gas is likely to be accompanied by a regulatory system concerned with the evaluation and approval of gas tariffs. Similarly, denationalization of electricity generation may be accompanied by some form of regulation of the tariff which would apply for sales to the transmission authority. The Government can be expected to review and assess the regulatory systems operating in other countries, and especially in the US (Fox 1984), before choosing a system for the UK. It is thus pertinent to consider some of the lessons which can be learned from the US experience.

One of the fundamental problems which has been learned is that regulation tends to spawn regulation, and hence the regulatory framework is likely to grow over time. Another lesson is that regulation can be associated with relatively slow decision-taking.[9] The establishment of a regulatory system leads to the growth of an associated bureaucracy, both within and external to the utility being regulated. If these effects were to occur in the UK they would be very important, since a principal non-political objective for privatization is said to be the promotion of competition and the generation of efficiency gains (gains from an improved allocation of resources) with the denationalized industries being more responsive to consumers' wishes. Clearly the measurement of any such gains must be net of any efficiency losses associated with regulation.[10]

An important source of efficiency losses has received considerable attention in both the theoretical and empirical literature relating to regulation in the US. This concerns control over the rate of return which regulated utilities are permitted to earn. Two important articles have shown that, irrespective of whether the regulated utility seeks to maximize profits or sales, the introduction of rate of return regulation will tend to cause efficiency losses. Averch and Johnson (1962) showed that a profit maximizing utility subject to rate of return regulation will tend to use a capital-labour ratio greater than that which minimizes costs for a given level of output when the allowed rate of return 's' exceeds the cost of capital 'r'. They also showed that if $r = s$, then all possible capital-labour ratios are equally profitable. In both cases, the firm has no incentive to minimize costs. In a subsequent article, Bailey and Malone (1970) showed that the Averch-Johnson effect is reversed if the utility has a sales maximization objective. That is, if $s > r$ then the sales maximizing utility will have an incentive to under invest and thus its chosen capital-labour ratio will be less than the cost minimizing ratio for the chosen output level.[11] The Averch-Johnson effect has been given empirical support in a number of studies (Courville 1974; Petersen 1975).

Recent empirical evidence has shown that the average rate of return on equity in electricity utilities in the US has, since 1973, been lower (on average by 4 percentage points) than that on industrials. Kahn (1983) has pointed out that this is likely to lead to a deterioration in the quality of service offered by electricity utilities. He quotes a study by National Economic Research Associates which shows a strong correlation between (with a lag) the availability[12] of coal-fired plants and earned rates of return, relatively high rates being associated with relatively high availability and vice versa. This evidence is also very relevant for the setting of a regulatory system in the UK.

An important objective of regulation is generally to control both the structure and level of utility prices. In recent years, federal regulation in the US has been concerned with promoting pricing structures related to marginal costs, in a similar manner to the recommendations contained in some of the UK White Papers on the nationalized industries (Treasury 1967). It has been estimated that in the early 1980s at least one half of a typical hearing on utility rates was devoted to questions of rate design. This is partly due to the Public Utilities Regulatory Policies Act (PURPA) of 1978. Among other things, this Act required each state to consider marginal cost pricing, peak load pricing and lifeline tariffs. Given the similar requirements of some aspects of the UK White Papers and PURPA, it is clearly important to consider which is likely to be the more effective in promoting a more efficient allocation of resources. It is to be hoped that the Government will consider these issues before denationalization occurs.

In this context, it is worth considering one other recent addition to the literature on regulation. Casual observation shows that publicly owned electricity utilities (such as *Electricité de France*) have been the pacemakers with regard to designing tariffs to reflect marginal costs. Such observation also shows that electricity utilities in the US which are subject to regulation have been slow to adopt such tariff systems, hence the prodding of PURPA. Sherman (1983) has argued that this slow response, and the potential inefficiency in resource allocation which accompanies it, is due to the rate of return regulation of the electricity utilities. He has also shown that rate of return regulation reduces the incentive for electricity utilities to adopt time-of-day tariffs.

It is thus clear that great care will have to be taken in the design of any regulatory system in the UK if efficiency losses due to failure to minimize costs are to be avoided.[13] It is also important to remember that these losses must be added to those resulting from compliance costs and from additional bureaucracy.

The evidence from the US appears to show quite conclusively that regulation of public utilities will be accompanied by losses associated with an inefficient allocation of resources, with relatively high compliance costs and with relatively slow decision-taking. In these circumstances, it is not surprising that there is increasing pressure in the US for deregulation.

Conclusion

This chapter has been concerned with various broadly defined administrative and procedural issues. The main focus has been directed at the possible privatization of the electricity and gas supply industries in the form recently considered by the Financial Secretary to the Treasury, that is denationalization of power stations, gas production and marketing. The chapter has argued that it is important to distinguish between the sale of existing power stations and the construction of new power stations funded by private investors, and questioned the likely attractiveness of the latter. It has also examined whether privately owned power stations could be operated to meet the national demand for electricity at least cost. Two problems were identified: first, the least cost operation of plants in merit order and, second, the choice of the optimal plant mix. In both cases, meeting demand at least cost would require investors to delegate control over the use made of power stations and the selection of new investment projects. The major problems with the privatization of the gas industry are likely to concern the denationalization of gas marketing operations, which is likely to encounter similar problems with regard to safety and union opposition as have delayed the proposed sale of gas showrooms.

Irrespective of how the electricity and gas industries are privatized, it is likely that privatization will be accompanied by the introduction of a system of regulation. A brief review of relevant experience in the US suggests that regulation is likely to lead to welfare losses arising from inefficiency in the allocation of resources, to increased bureaucracy and delays in taking decisions, and possibly to relatively high compliance costs. This review is sufficient to show that denationalization will not necessarily overcome the problems with the control of nationalized industries which have concerned successive British governments. The fundamental problems concerned with the control of public utilities are very similar, irrespective of whether they are in the public or private sectors.

Finally, an implication of the discussion presented in this chapter is that very careful attention should be given to the best form of denationalization of the electricity and gas industries if, as seems likely, this does occur. It is believed that the main options which are being considered are keeping the industries intact but selling 51% of their equity (as in the case of BT) and having vertical disintegration with the denationalization of segments of the industries. It seems evident that hasty decisions are unlikely to lead to the net increase of economic benefits over costs which many protagonists of privatization see as its *raison d'être.* The analysis suggests that any act of privatization of the gas and electricity industries which is accompanied by regulation will generate both benefits and costs. It is thus important to consider the trade-off between these benefits and costs with reference to the status quo position given by the existing nationalized electricity and gas industries.

NOTES

1 The definition of a natural monopoly poses many problems. It is commonly considered to apply to industries where competition between many firms would be unstable and would give way to a monopoly, because of the existence of substantial economies of scale. In this situation the alternatives are public ownership or private ownership with regulation. The relevance of the natural monopoly argument to nationalized industries, including electricity and gas supply, has recently been discussed by Beesley and Littlechild (1983).

2 BNOC's activities as defined by the Submarine and Pipe-lines Act are described in *The British National Oil Corporation* (BNOC undated).

3 The figures quoted in the text do not reflect the final bid made by the Dorset Group following the changes made to company taxation in the 1984 Budget. The figures given in the text are comparable, whereas the latest figure is not comparable with BGC's 1983 valuation.

4 In March 1983, the CEGB owned 100 power stations.

5 The potential market values of nationalized industries which might be denationalized have recently been estimated by Osborne and Costello (1984). The electricity supply industry was valued at between £3,500m. and £4,500m. The basis of this valuation is not understood, but appears to result in a low valuation.

6 The CEGB's planning modules, including the planning suite, SYMAN, are described in Monopolies and Mergers Commission (1981b).

7 The market value of an asset is related to its expected future earnings. To express these earnings as a single sum it is necessary to remove the time dimension and make them appear as if they were all realized at a single date. This can be done by calculating their present value, which varies inversely with the size of the rate of discount. Public and private sector firms tend to use different discount rates. Since 1978, nationalized industries have, in some circumstances, been required to use a real rate of 5%. Oil companies operating in the North Sea often use real rates of 12-15%.

8 The implications for equity of denationalization at relatively low market values are discussed in Webb (1984b).

9 Some of the costs of regulation with respect to surface transport have been estimated by Moore (1975).

10 On 17 February 1981, President Reagan signed Executive Order 12291 which required all regulations to be submitted to the Office of Manpower and Budget for review, and required regulations to be established which would maximize net social benefits to the extent permitted by law. The annual benefits and costs must therefore be estimated for the purpose of compiling a regulatory budget. See Tozzi and Clarke (1983).

11 It should be obvious that the case where $s < r$ is not interesting since the utility would not then invest in capital projects.

12 The availability of a power station is a measure of the number of hours a year that it is available for operation. Other things being equal, low availability is likely to be associated with higher risk of power failures.

13 It is interesting to note that concern about differential rates of return earned in the public and private sectors was one of the principal justifications for the introduction of financial targets in the 1961 White Paper on nationalized industries (Treasury 1961).

7

Government and the New Hybrids

David Steel

Introduction

In support of the privatization programme, ministers frequently claim that public enterprises which can be denationalized will thereby be freed from 'the dead hand of the public sector'. In particular, they point to the failure of successive attempts to establish a satisfactory framework of relations between government and the nationalized industries and argue that ministerial intervention (for example, in support of macroeconomic and political objectives) can only be excluded by denationalization. The aim of this chapter is, first, to assess whether denationalization of itself is likely to have this effect and to explore the uneasy linkages between the sale of enterprises and measures of liberalization which extend the scope of competition. Second, it will examine some of the administrative and legal implications should intervention occur in those cases in which less than 100% of the shares are sold.

A significant feature of the denationalization element in the first Thatcher Government's privatization programme was that in the most important cases it was only partial (Steel and Heald 1984b). Earlier denationalizations, such as steel and road haulage in the 1950s, were outright in the sense that public assets were simply sold to private bidders. On this occasion, however, the entire assets of an enterprise or all of its shares were sold only in a few instances, such as AI, most of BR's hotels and some of the NEB's subsidiaries. Instead, the standard approach was to convert the organization (usually a public corporation) into a Companies Act company and then to introduce private capital by the sale of roughly 50% of the shares, thus creating a hybrid company. (In broad terms, hybrids can be defined as companies in which there exist substantial public and private shareholdings.) What was remarkable was the almost total absence of discussion of the implications of different levels of government shareholding for either the exercise of public control or the hybrid's operational autonomy. Nevertheless, this model was adopted for BAe, C&W, Britoil and ABP, and was prescribed for BA and BT. However, the Government never provided a coherent justification of its decision to retain a substantial stake or of the appropriate level. There seemed to be a presumption in favour of 50% but the number was set just below so that the Treasury could justify the enterprise's subsequent exclusion from the PSBR.

The discussion so far has been deliberately couched in the past tense because it now seems likely that there will be an important discontinuity between the policies of the first and second terms of Mrs Thatcher's Government. The privatization programme was initiated in 1979 without any official blueprint, due in part to the limited commitments and low-key tone of the 1979 Conservative manifesto. Given the necessity to secure parliamentary approval for complex legislation, progress in implementation was predictably slow. By 1981, many commentators, even some sympathetic to the programme, were becoming rather dismissive about the lack of practical achievements and seriously underestimated the groundwork which had been done. In the event, the programme did not run out of steam but acquired new momentum, initially because it provided a unifying theme for a Conservative Party deeply divided on macroeconomic policy and, later, from the post-Falklands realization that the Government would win a second term. Subsequently, the 1983 Conservative manifesto struck a much more confident note about the success and future potential of the programme, to be followed by Mr John Moore's ambitious new agenda (Moore 1983) and the £10bn. target for asset sales during the Government's second term. Then, during the 1984 Budget debate, Mr Peter Rees, the Chief Secretary to the Treasury, announced that it was the Government's intention to dispose of all its 'residual shareholdings' when the opportunities arose (Rees 1984).

Given the extent to which the hybrid had become the chosen method of denationalization, the term 'residual shareholding' is itself significant for it scarcely carries any sense of deliberate choice or permanence. It is therefore necessary to deal with one argument which has been adduced to deny the importance of the issues raised in this chapter and in Steel (1984). Ministers have argued that hybrid status is not a destination to be reached but only an intermediate station on the route to full denationalization. In support of this view, they point to the limits on the capital market's ability to absorb large flotations and to the difficulties of fixing the prices at which shares should be offered. Both these considerations are said to favour moving in stages rather than selling all the shares at once. Even before the Rees statement, the re-elected Government had halved its shareholding in C&W from 46% to 23% and then quickly followed that announcement by selling all its remaining 49% stake in ABP in April 1984. Given these developments, it has been argued that the 'unresolved questions' relating to hybrids are merely of 'academic' and passing interest, but of no substantive importance.

Undeniably, both the logic and rhetoric of the Government's arguments have always pointed towards total, not partial, denationalization. Moreover, Stephen Littlechild (1981, 14), one of the leading advocates of privatization, has argued that joint ownership can only be useful as a transitional measure: '... as long as ultimate control lies with government, one cannot realistically hope to avoid all the problems'. His comment, however, was prompted by the Government's reliance upon the hybrid model for there was little in 1981 to suggest that it planned to divest itself completely. The discontinuity in policy evolution ought to be recognized, not obscured. Although the pragmatic arguments about the novelty of the operations and the limitations on the capital market's absorptive capacity have some substance, it is merely a convenient rationalization to claim that they satisfactorily explain the creation of a new generation of hybrids. Not least, only Britoil involved an exceptionally large issue and much of the financial comment related to the uncertainties generated by the government shareholdings.

There are three reasons why 'hybridity' remains of interest, even after Mr Rees' statement. First, it is an appropriate topic for academic study (in the scholarly rather than pejorative sense) to consider why the hybrid company became the vehicle for a radical programme of denationalization. Second, even if hybridity is only transitional, for some enterprises it is likely to hold for a number of years. If there is anything in the argument about the capacity of the capital market, this is going to be a much more serious constraint in the future as the 'giants' such as BT and possibly BGC and the ESI come to be sold. Moreover, it is not clear whether this statement applies only to existing hybrids or to prospective hybrids as well. In the parliamentary debates on the legislation providing for the denationalization of public corporations such as BAe, ministers did in fact point to the public shareholding as a safeguard for the national interest. Enterprises whose activities are significant for the performance of the economy as a whole are likely to take the form of hybrids for a period of time which is both considerable and uncertain in length. The Conservative Government would need a third term in order to complete the programme as it has been redefined and extended. There is also the possibility that, following the next general election, a different government might decide to retain the hybrids either to avoid further disruption or because the financial costs of renationalization were deemed prohibitive.

The third point is more indirect, but equally important. Although *part* of the analysis of this chapter is dependent upon a continuing government shareholding, *some* of the issues identified would persist even after full denationalization of at least *some* of the enterprises. The existence of a public shareholding is significant as a spur to ministerial involvement and will make it more difficult for them to deny responsibility. Crucially, however, it is not the only ground for believing that in many cases relations are likely to be closer than ministers currently intend. A careful examination of the government-hybrid relationship thus affords access to the issues which emerge when public ownership gives way to public regulation.

The Government's Position

In Parliament and in the offers for sale, ministers have repeatedly declared their intention not to intervene in the commercial affairs of hybrid companies. At the despatch box, there have been few qualifications but in the prospectuses there has been greater caution. For example, the Britoil prospectus reproduced the text of a letter dated 9 November 1982 to the Chairman, of which the following paragraph was part:

> HM Government does *not intend* to use its rights as an Ordinary Shareholder to intervene in the commercial decisions of the Company. It might however wish in the relevant circumstances to use its voting rights as an Ordinary Shareholder in conjunction with the temporarily enhanced voting rights of the Special Share to ensure that control of the Company remained in the hands of an independent Board of Directors. It does *not expect* to vote its shareholding in opposition to a resolution supported by a majority of the Board in other circumstances, although it *retains the power to do so* (Britoil 1982, 17, my italics).

Ministers insist that the new hybrids will be treated just like any other private sector company. Having been released from the troublesome connection between public corporation and Exchequer finances (Steel and Heald 1984a), the managerial decisions of the hybrids will not be overridden by Treasury decisions in support of macroeconomic policy. Moreover, it is contended that the existence of private shareholders, and the consequent disciplines of the capital market, will make it more difficult for governments to intervene for any purpose, thus affording the hybrids with an insulation from political pressures never enjoyed by nationalized industries. The Government, therefore, sees its role as an absentee or, at most, as a largely inactive institutional shareholder.

The only exception to this position concerns takeovers. In the case of BAe, ministers indicated that they would mobilize their shareholding to forestall an attempt to alter the articles of association which limit the extent of foreign ownership. The self-denying ordinance quoted above from the Britoil prospectus specifically mentioned maintaining the Company's 'independence' as a situation in which the shareholding might be voted. Ironically, the shareholding is largely superfluous in this situation because the Government also owns a 'Special Share' which can be invoked to outvote all the other shares (but only in strictly defined circumstances, principally relating to takeover). Special shares exist in Britoil and C&W, and even in AI where the entire shareholding was sold immediately. Although these Special Shares are therefore separate from the question of hybridity, they remain of considerable significance because of the way in which the threat of takeover is one of the mechanisms of capital market discipline.

Attempts to generalize about the hybrids inevitably run into the fact that the enterprises involved so far are a rather mixed bag, varying considerably in terms of size and economic significance. Each one is in many ways a special case and its future relationship with government will be influenced by factors such as its business history and location in the economy. This diversity is one possible explanation for the variations in the constitutions of the new hybrids. However, they can more convincingly be interpreted as a reflection of the pragmatism that is characteristic of the British approach to the establishment of institutions. In this case, departments appear to have been left to make their own decisions on matters of detail, with the Treasury in its role as policy co-ordinator not being able or wishing to achieve a degree of uniformity. These variations extend to questions which might have been thought to involve matters of significant principle: such as whether there should be government directors (on Britoil but not ABP) and whether there should be statutory restrictions on increases in the government shareholding (for BAe but not BA). Such variations in the enterprises themselves and in their constitutions make the search for generalization hazardous but nonetheless essential.

The Viability of the Government's Position

In support of their policy of non-intervention, ministers have on a number of occasions cited the precedent of BP. The relevance of this precedent, however, is questionable. The experience of BP is largely a result of the special circumstances surrounding its acquisition in 1914, its market position and its financial success, all of which have enabled it to behave much as any other large British mutinational company and to be treated as such by governments and by its customers. Some of these factors apply to certain of the new hybrids but by no means to all of them. Indeed, BP's experience highlights the significance of the distinction between the denationalization and liberalization arms of the Government's programme (Steel and Heald 1984b). Competition does provide a degree of insulation from government intervention because its costs cannot be passed on to consumers.[1] If denationalization were merely to result in the substitution of private for public monopoly, the existence of private shareholders alone is unlikely to provide much insulation.

However, references to BP have drawn attention to how little is known about the reality of its past relationships with governments (for example, what the government directors actually did). Corti and Frazer's (1983) account of the origins and growth of BNOC contains a number of stinging asides about BP's role, notably its refusal to guarantee the security of British oil supplies during the 1973 OPEC oil crisis, its aggressive opposition to participation agreements, and its jealousy of its traditional role as adviser on oil policy to British governments. Even allowing for the authors' obvious loyalties, their comments cast doubts upon whether BP's autonomy was accompanied by much accountability to its majority owner. Of possible wider relevance is BP's tactic of looking both ways, treating its government shareholding as a nuisance but exploiting it commercially.

As far as most of the new hybrids are concerned, it seems likely that even the present Government will come under pressure to intervene to a greater extent than is currently envisaged. This can perhaps be best illustrated by considering a series of hypothetical questions:

(i) despite ministers' insistence that the hybrids are not backed by the Exchequer, what would be their response were one of them to go bankrupt?

(ii) were BR or some of the energy undertakings to be denationalized, would the Department of Transport take no interest in rail electrification, and the Department of Energy cease to be concerned with depletion profiles and nuclear power station technology and development?

(iii) would the present Government allow a hybrid to curtail drastically rural services on the grounds that cross-subsidization was no longer feasible? If, in order to preserve the existing network of services, it decided to provide explicit subsidies, would it not take a close interest in the manner in which they were calculated and spent?

(iv) what would be the Government's response were a major hybrid, such as BT, to abandon its current British suppliers (whose market share is in any case threatened by liberalization)?

(v) especially in relation to public utilities where industrial action can disrupt the entire economy, would ministers be able to keep out of major disputes?

The history of ministerial 'self-denying ordinances', for instance in relation to the nationalized industries or to the provision of financial support for 'lame ducks', suggests that they tend to be forgotten under pressures such as those indicated by these questions.[2] Quite apart from their own appreciation of the political consequences of non-intervention, of which members of the present Cabinet have on occasion shown themselves aware (for example, the Ravenscraig closure decision), ministers' resolve not to intervene will be challenged by select committees and by MPs generally. In particular, they are likely to be confronted by the argument, probably spearheaded by the PAC, that there remains a large public financial stake for which there is no accountability. In the past, the PAC has sought on this ground to obtain greater access to the books of earlier hybrids (for example, the subsidiaries of the NEB) and it has already urged ministers to take a closer interest in the affairs of BAe because of the public money at stake in relation to the Airbus project (PAC 1982).

The fact that the new generation of hybrids, unlike their predecessors including BP, have been in full public ownership has given rise to expectations among MPs and the media about access and influence on the part of ministers. Irrespective of whether formal access is granted — which at present seems most unlikely — such pressure will increase the amount of interest taken by departments in the affairs of hybrids falling within their functional remit. MPs will be able to inquire why the government shareholding has not been mobilized to secure various ends and will question ministers about the action or inaction of government directors. In the past, MPs have shown themselves to be adept at exploiting the 'non-use of ministerial powers' tactic to open up areas which governments seek to keep closed by denying any responsibility. Ministers have also frequently succumbed, initially asking boards for information and then moving on to make suggestions and to begin applying informal pressure.

Another source of pressure upon ministers to intervene is likely to be other governments. Several of the hybrids operate in markets in which agreements between governments are crucially important. Distinctions between governmental and commercial responsibilities are not always clearly delineated. Moreover, the attitude of other governments towards these companies will be influenced by the fact that they would still be classified as public enterprises on the basis of the definitions conventionally applied in international comparisons. In these circumstances, it would be extremely difficult for the Government to stand aside were C&W or BAe, for example, to default on contracts with foreign governments. Equally, in the telecommunications field, there are doubts as to whether a private sector undertaking can participate in discussions and negotiations which hitherto have been conducted on a government-to-government basis. Thus, even if ministers are strong-minded enough not to succumb to the temptation to intervene in the sort of circumstances outlined earlier, they may find themselves compelled to become more involved in order to avoid embarrassing friction with either the PAC or with other governments. In neither case would ministerial denials of any responsibility seem credible in view of the scale of the government shareholding. It is important, however, to stress again that intervention is much more likely to occur in relation to certain hybrids than others.

This point is clearly illustrated by BT. As a result of its size, its sensitive position economically and socially, and its dominant market position even after liberalization, ministers have had to acknowledge that BT must be subject to some public control. Since partial denationalization was first announced two years ago, there has been a steady growth in the scope and intensity of the regulatory framework that is to be applied. A long and complex licence (Department of Trade & Industry 1984) will determine the terms under which BT operates and a new office, OFTEL, is being established to police the system, whose Director General is intended to be independent. Based upon US experience, there has been some discussion as to whether he is liable to be 'captured' by BT. It is just as likely, however, that he will be 'leaned upon' by ministers and, in the British system of government, it is not possible to provide even the degree of insulation from such pressure that is afforded by the formal separation of powers in the US. The new regime that is being constructed for telecommunications in Britain is the subject of John Kay's chapter in this book. Here, it is sufficient only to note that ministers have been driven to accept that BT cannot be regarded as just an ordinary, large private sector company. Whilst it is clearly unique among the present generation of hybrids, some of the factors which have led ministers to this conclusion in this case are of wider application. If, as recent ministerial speeches have indicated, the denationalization programme gathers momentum and extends to other public utilities, similar considerations will apply.

So far, this analysis has concentrated upon the position of the present Government, which is strongly disposed *not* to intervene in the running of the hybrids which it is in the process of creating. Its successors, whatever their political complexion, will not be bound by its declarations of intent, and may decide that they wish to become an active shareholder and/or to exert informal pressure upon the boards of these undertakings. Given the scale of the government shareholding, there is no doubt that they would be able to take control if they chose to do so. It would be difficult for a government to be outvoted in C&W where it now holds only 23% of the shares; it would be impossible for this to happen in the majority of cases where it holds just under 50% of the shares. Thus, even if the present Government succeeds in maintaining its non-interventionist stance, the question of relationships between ministers and hybrid companies remains an important one.

Some Implications of Intervention in Hybrid Companies

The conclusion of the analysis presented in the last section is that relations between ministers and hybrid companies — and in some cases even with fully denationalized ones — will be much closer than is currently envisaged. As far as hybrid companies are concerned, such a development would raise a number of important issues. First, there is the question of the legality of ministerial intervention in view of the declarations that have been included in all the offers for sale. The legal issues involved in this area are complex, especially for a student of public administration with no expertise in company law. In theory, aggrieved shareholders could take legal action on the basis that they had suffered loss through breach of contract upon the part of the Government. In practice, however, such a claim would be extremely difficult to sustain, not least because the Government has worded its declarations of intent in such a manner as to keep its options wide open. Thus, the relevant part of the Britoil prospectus includes the qualification that the Government 'retains the power' to invoke its rights as a shareholder. Moreover, the fact that the Government did not feel inhibited from reducing its holding in C&W to 23% within two years of stating in the original prospectus that it intended 'to maintain a majority shareholding for the forseeable future' suggests that the force of such declarations is not very strong.

In the unlikely event that ministers felt that there was a serious risk of their action being challenged successfully in the courts, they could legislate to grant themselves indemnity. It seems, therefore, that there is no serious legal constraint upon ministerial intervention. Much more significant as a restraint will be practical considerations, such as the effect that such intervention might have upon the company's rating on the stock market and upon a government's reputation as an honest broker, especially within the financial community in both the UK and overseas. In both cases, the impact of intervention upon the hybrid's financial position would be crucial. Frequently, it is likely to have an adverse effect, as for example when a hybrid is induced to maintain uneconomic services or to accept an uncompetitive tender in order to provide jobs in particular areas, but there is no reason why government intervention should not in certain circumstances act as a spur to greater efficiency and lead to an improvement in the standing of the company (unless one subscribes to an extreme version of the 'public bad, private good' doctrine).

If ministers decide to intervene in the affairs of a hybrid, they can achieve this end by mobilizing their shareholding. However, this would be very much a last resort. The company's directors would be well aware of the latent power of such a large block of voting shares — one suspects that even now they are conscious of the fact that their largest shareholder is only sleeping, not deceased — and would consider it prudent to listen carefully to ministers' views. Moreover, a government would be in a strong position to influence board appointments. On specific issues, ministers could resort to the practice of persuasion and arm-twisting which they have adopted on many occasions in relation to the nationalized industries.

Such pressure would normally be exerted upon the hybrid's chairman rather than through those directors who are government nominees. The present Government's attitude towards such directors appears to be rather ambivalent. They have been appointed in some cases (for example, Britoil and BAe) but not others (for example, ABP), with no satisfactory explanation being offered for the difference in treatment. Nor do the appointments that have been made indicate an intention that their role is to act as delegates, or even as representatives, of ministers. In any case, their legal position — a director's formal duty is to the company as a whole rather than to the group of shareholders who nominated him or her — would make it difficult for them to push the Government's line in board deliberations. At present, they do not appear to act even as a channel of communication between the board and Whitehall (and again it might be difficult for them to disclose board papers and discussions at a stage at which this would be helpful). Government directors on the boards of hybrids are thus in a completely different position from that of the civil servants who sat on the boards of certain nationalized industries during the 1970s.

Possibly the greatest danger in the present situation is that practice will evolve in a piecemeal manner. Ministers will start to become more involved and they will do so in a variety of different ways. Parliament will gradually become aware of what is going on but it will already be too late for it to have much influence. The way in which the regulatory framework for BT has emerged, such that even at this late stage no one is quite sure what kind of animal is being created, is widely regarded as unsatisfactory. But at least in this case there has been some public discussion of the issues involved. In relation to the other hybrids, there has been virtually nothing. The inevitable result will be confusion and a blurring of accountability.

Such an outcome would accord with the pragmatic approach to constitutional and administrative matters that is favoured in the UK. Those familiar with the experience of the nationalized industries may also feel that there is no alternative. However, there was extensive debate prior to the establishment of public corporations, following which certain ground rules were agreed and enshrined in statute, and three attempts (Treasury 1961; 1967; 1978) have been made to codify financial relationships with government. Given its present attitude, the Government is most unlikely to accept the need for anything similar in relation to hybrid companies (but see Steel 1984 for such a suggestion). The danger, however, is that the very situation that ministers are seeking to eradicate by partly denationalizing public enterprises will return and that it may be even more damaging to enterprise health and to the principle of accountability for public funds because of the complete absence of a framework governing their relations with hybrid companies.

Is Hybridity the Real Issue?

In several senses, this chapter has been exploring uncharted territory. Prior to 1979, hybrid enterprises were rare in the UK and the only major precedent — BP — provides little guidance for the present generation. As far as these enterprises are concerned, it is much too soon to be able to gauge whether the predictions of this chapter will be fulfilled. Neither is it possible yet to detect a clear pattern of government-hybrid relationships. The procedures traditionally associated with the *sponsorship* role have been terminated, to be replaced by what has become known as the *stewardship* of the government shareholding. Given the Government's self-denying ordinances, there seems to be uncertainty on all sides as to what this entails.

Ministers claim that the relationship now is no different from that which they maintain with equivalent private sector companies, but such assurances should be treated with scepticism. First, all of the hybrids operate in areas in which government retains major responsibilities and there is little evidence on public record to document departmental contacts with wholly private sector companies when their activities impinge upon public policy concerns. In the perhaps exceptional case of oil, these contacts are extensive, mainly because of the licensing system, but parallels may develop as the hybrid model is extended to the public utilities. Second, meetings between ministers and chairmen, and at official level, are likely to have implicit as well as explicit agendas. The government side will be constrained by the ambiguities of the stewardship role, but will be anxious to acclaim evidence that denationalization has been a 'success'. The hybrid will be more ambivalent still: wanting to keep its massively dominant shareholder well-informed without disturbing its inactivity; wondering about the size and timing of future reductions in that shareholding which impinge upon its own ability to raise equity finance; and wishing to be an acknowledged success without being drawn too deeply into political controversies about later denationalizations.

Given the Government's attitude towards public sector organizations, it is perhaps unsurprising that the hybrids have readily agreed to being labelled as part of the private sector. Similarly, as the uncertainties surrounding their relationship with (future) governments have been identified, they have begun to anticipate the sale of the remaining government shareholding, with equanimity if not satisfaction. For example, the chairman of ABP welcomed the second sale in confident and positive terms.

However, sale of the 'residual' government shareholding will not dispose of all of the questions raised in this chapter. Many of the enterprises involved are not, and cannot be, regarded as ordinary private companies. In most cases, the Government is committed, either through a 'Special Share' or by other means, to preserving the enterprises' independence. Regardless of how it seeks to achieve this end, the point here is that such a restriction upon takeover curtails one of the main mechanisms of capital market discipline. Moreover, many of the enterprises operate in fields in which legitimate public policy issues would still arise. As long as governments accept any responsibility for defence, energy or transport, for example, denationalization will not — and should not — eliminate all ministerial and parliamentary intervention.

The argument of this chapter, therefore, is that for most of the enterprises involved in the denationalization programme the question of future relationships with government cannot just be 'defined' away and is deserving of much greater attention than it has received to date in either official or academic circles. As far as the latter are concerned, research in this area is made rather complex by the fact that it calls for expertise in at the very least public administration, constitutional and administrative law, company law, and economics. However, it is a task of considerable importance, both to the enterprises themselves and to the shareholders and taxpayers whose funds — voluntarily or involuntarily — are at stake.

NOTES

1 Competition is not always sufficient to block intervention. When enterprises faced by international competition are subject to intervention on plant location and closures, the effects can be debilitating, as the experience of the European steel industry illustrates very clearly (see, for example, *Annals of Public and Co-operative Economy* 1980).

2 To date, the most publicized case involving a hybrid has been Britoil's decision to cancel its oil rig order with Scott Lithgow on the Clyde. Although there was no direct Government intervention in Britoil's decision, a considerable sum of public money was provided for the consequent rescue of the shipyard.

Bibliography

Annals of Public and Co-operative Economy. 1980. Steel and the state in Europe. Vol. 51, 371-544.

Averch, H. and L. L. Johnson. 1962. Behaviour of the firm under regulatory constraint, *American Economic Review* 52, 1052-1069.

Bagwell, P. S. 1984. *End of the line? The fate of British Railways under Thatcher.* London: Verso.

Bailey, E. and J. C. Malone. 1970. Resource allocation and the regulated firm, *Bell Journal of Economics and Management Science* 1, 129-142.

Batstone, E., A. Ferner and M. Terry. 1984. *Consent and efficiency: labour relations and management strategy in the state enterprise.* Oxford: Blackwell.

Beesley, M. E. 1981. *Liberalisation of the use of British Telecommunications network.* London: HMSO.

___ and S. C. Littlechild. 1983. Privatisation: principles, problems and priorities, *Lloyds Bank Review* No. 149, 1-20.

BNOC (undated). *The British National Oil Corporation.* Glasgow BNOC.

Britoil. 1982. *Offer for sale of ordinary shares.* London: Britoil.

BT. 1984. *Half-yearly figures and changes in accounting policies.* News Release PB42, 30 March.

BTUC. 1983. *The American experience.* London: BTUC

___. 1984. *The battle for British Telecom.* London BTUC. 1983.

Butler, A. 1979. Speech given at a luncheon for Aldridge and Brownhills businessmen on 14 December 1979.

Corti, G. and F. Frazer. 1983. *The nation's oil: a story of control.* London: Graham & Trotman.

Courville, L. 1974. Regulation and efficiency in the electric utility industry, *Bell Journal of Economics and Management Science* 5, 53-74.

Daniel, W. W. and N. Millward. 1983. *Workplace industrial relations in Britain: the DE/PSI/SSRC survey.* London: Heinemann.

Danielsen, A. L. and D. R. Kamerschen (eds.). 1983. *Current issues in public-utility economics.* Lexington, Mass.: Lexington Books, D.C. Heath.

Davis, J. 1983. Little profit for City advisers: the great state sell-off, *The Times,* 6 October 1983.

Deloitte, Haskins & Sells. 1983. *British gas efficiency study for the British Gas Corporation and the Department of Energy.* London: Deloitte, Haskins & Sells.

DI. 1982. *The future of telecommunications in Britain.* Cmnd. 8610. London: HMSO.

DTI. 1984. *The British Telecom Licence:* Licence granted by the Secretary of State for Trade and Industry to British Telecommunications under section 7 of the Telecommunications Act 1984.
London: HMSO.

The Economist. 1978. Appomatox or civil war? 27 May, 20-21.

___. 1982. Thatcher's think-tank takes aim at the welfare state, 18 September, 25-26.

___. 1984. British Gas: Possession or Wytchcraft? 3 March, 32.

Foster, C. D. 1984. Privatising British airports: what's to be gained? *Public Money* 3, No. 4, 19-23.

Foster, N., S. G. B. Henry and C. Trinder. 1984. Public and private sector pay: a partly disaggregated study, *National Institute Economic Review* 107, 63-73.

Fowler, N. 1977. *The right track.* London: Conservative Party.

Fox, W. 1984. *Federal regulation of energy.* Colorado Springs: McGraw-Hill.

Friedman, M. 1980. 'Memorandum', in Treasury and Civil Service Committee *Memoranda on monetary policy.* HC 720 of Session 1979-80. London: HMSO.

Heald, D. A. 1983. *Public expenditure: its defence and reform.* Oxford: Martin Robertson.

___. 1984. Privatisation: analysing its appeal and limitations, *Fiscal Studies* 5,No. 1, 36-46.

___ and D. R. Steel. 1981. Privatisation of UK public enterprises, *Annals of Public and Co-operative Economy* 52, 351-367.

___ and D. R. Steel. 1982. Privatising public enterprise: an analysis of the Government's case, *Political Quarterly* 53, 333-349.

Henderson, P. D. 1977. Two British errors: their probable size and some possible lessons, *Oxford Economic Papers* 29, 159-205.
Hepple, B. A. 1982. The Transfer of Undertakings (Protection of Employment) Regulations, *Industrial Law Journal* 12, 29-40.
Hills, J. 1984. What is the public sector worth?, *Fiscal Studies* 5, No. 1, 18-31.
Howe, Sir Geoffrey. 1981. Speech to the Selsdon Group, 1 July 1981, Conservative Central Office Press Release 533/81.
Imber, V. and P. Todd. 1983. Public expenditure: definitions and trends, *Economic Trends* No. 361, November, 138-51.
Incomes Data Report. 1983a. No. 393, 18.
___. 1983b. No. 414, 13.
Industry and Trade Committee. 1982. *Inquiry into cable expansion and broadcasting policy.* Cmnd. 8679. London: HMSO.
___. 1983. *The British Steel Corporation's prospects.* HC 212 of session 1982-83. London: HMSO.
Johnson, C. 1983. Privatisation's progress, *Lloyds Bank Economic Bulletin* No. 60, December 1983, 1-3.
Kahn, A. E. 1983. 'Utility regulation revisited', in A. L. Danielsen and D. R. Kamerschen (eds.). op. cit.
Kay, J. A. and Z. A. Silberston. 1984. The new industrial policy — privatization and competition, *Midland Bank Review,* Spring 1984, 8-16.
Labour Party. 1983. *New hope for Britain.* London: Labour Party.
Labour Party — TUC-CSEU. 1972. *Nationalisation of shipbuilding, ship-repair and marine engineering.* London: Labour Party.
Labour Research. 1983. Docking out of public ports. Vol. 72, 307.
Likierman, A. 1983. Evidence on accusations of manipulating profitability: adjustments for inflation by the nationalised industries 1976-81, *Accounting and Business Research* 14, Winter, 29-34.
___. 1984. Privatisation proceeds hand in hand with self sufficiency, *Public Finance and Accountancy,* April 1984, 17-18.
Littlechild, S. C. 1981. Ten steps to denationalisation, *Journal of Economic Affairs* 2, 11-19.
___. 1983. *Regulation of British Telecommunications' profitability.* London: Department of Industry.
Lord, S. 1983. 'Gas and electricity shops', in S. Hastings and H. Levie (eds.) *Privatisation?* Nottingham: Spokesman.
MacLachlan, S. 1983. *The National Freight buy-out.* London: Macmillan.
Millward, R. 1982. 'The comparative performance of public and private ownership' in Lord Roll (ed.) *The Mixed Economy.* London: Macmillan.
MMC. 1979. *The supply of petrol in the United Kingdom by wholesale.* Cmnd. 7433. London: HMSO.
___. 1980. *Domestic gas appliances: a report on the supply of certain gas appliances in the United Kingdom.* HC 703 of session 1979-80. London: HMSO.
___. 1981a. *British Rail Hovercraft Limited and Hoverlloyd Limited: a report on the proposed merger.* HC 374 of session 1980-81. London: HMSO.
___. 1981b. *Central Electricity Generating Board: a report on the operation by the Board of its system for the generation and supply of electricity in bulk.* HC 315 of session 1980-81. London: HMSO.
___. 1983. *National Coal Board: a report on the efficiency and costs in the development, production and supply of coal by the NCB.* Cmnd. 8920 — I and II. London: HMSO.
Moore, J. 1983. Speech given to the annual conference of City of London Stockbrokers Fielding, Newson Smith at Plaisterer's Hall, London Wall on 1 November 1983, (Treasury Press Release 190/83).
___ .1984. Speech given to the Eccleston Supper Club on 18 July. Treasury Press Release 122/84.
Moore, T. G. 1975. 'Deregulating surface freight transport', in A. Phillips (ed.) *Promoting competition in regulated markets.* Washington: Brookings Institution.

NEDO. 1981. *Report of working party on nationalised industries' investment.* London: Mimeo, NEDC (81) 53.
NEDO. 1981. *Interdependence of the public and private sectors in the UK.* London: Mimeo, NEDC, (81) 25.
NICG. 1981. *Interdependence of the public and private sector businesses.* London: Mimeo, NEDC (81) 31.
NUM. 1983. *Hands off the pits — no privatisation of coal.* Sheffield: NUM.
NUR. 1984. *Privatisation,* presented to POEU's London Regional Council conference, January 1984. London: Mimeo, NUR.
Osborne, M. and M. Costello. 1984. Selling off the public estate: a broker's view, *Public Money* 3, 4, 57-59.
PAC. 1982. *Sale of shares in British Aerospace; sales of government shareholdings in other publicly owned companies and in British Petroleum Ltd; postponement of payments.* Tenth Report. HC 189 of session 1981-82. London: HMSO.
___. 1984. *Sale of government shareholdings in publicly owned companies.* Seventeenth Report. HC 443 of session 1983-84. London: HMSO.
Peacock, A. T. and G. K. Shaw. 1981. *The Public Sector Borrowing Requirement.* University College at Buckingham, Occasional Papers in Economics, No. 1.
Petersen, H. C. 1975. An empirical test of regulatory effects, *Bell Journal of Economics* 6, 111-126.
POEU. 1984. *The privatisation of British Telecom,* presented to POEU London Regional Council conference, January 1984. London: Mimeo, POEU.
Rees, P. 1984. *Hansard,* 14 March, col. 420.
ROFS. 1983. Annual Report 1982-83. London: HMSO.
Sherman, R. 1983. 'Is public utility regulation beyond hope?', in A. L. Danielsen and D. R. Kamerschen (eds.) op. cit.
Steel, D. R. 1984. Government and the new hybrids: a trail of unanswered questions, *Fiscal Studies* 5, No. 1, 87-97.
___ and D. A. Heald. 1984a. The integration of public enterprise and Exchequer finances: unravelling the damaging myths, *Public Administration* 62,337-348.
___. Forthcoming. 'The privatisation of public enterprises 1979-83', in P. M. Jackson (ed.) *RIPA Policy Initiatives Project.* London: RIPA.
Taylor, C. T. and A. R. Threadgold. 1979. *Real national saving and sectoral composition.* Bank of England Discussion Paper No. 6. London: Bank of England.
Tozzi, J. J. and E. H. Clarke. 1983. 'On information and the regulation of public utilities', in A. L. Danielsen and D. R. Kamerschen (eds.). op. cit.
Treasury. 1961. *The financial and economic obligations of the nationalised industries.* Cmnd. 1337. London: HMSO.
___. 1967. Nationalised industries: a review of economic and financial objectives. Cmnd. 3437. London: HMSO.
___. 1978. *The nationalised industries.* Cmnd. 7131. London: HMSO.
___. 1979a. *The Government's expenditure plans 1979-80 to 1982-83.* Cmnd. 7439. London: HMSO.
___. 1979b. *The Government's expenditure plans 1980-81.* Cmnd. 7746. London: HMSO.
___. 1980. *The Government's expenditure plans 1980-81 to 1983-84.* Cmnd. 7841. London: HMSO.
___. 1981. *The Government's expenditure plans 1981-82 to 1983-84.* Cmnd. 8175. London: HMSO.
___. 1982a. *The Government's expenditure plans 1982-83 to 1984-85.* Cmnd. 8494-I and II. London: HMSO.
___. 1982b. The public sector for the public, *Economic Progress Report* No. 145, May 1982, 1-4.
___. 1983. *The Government's expenditure plans 1983-84 to 1985-86.* Cmnd. 8789-I and II. London: HMSO.
___. 1984a. *The Government's expenditure plans 1984-85 to 1986-87.* Cmnd. 9143-I and II. London: HMSO.

___. 1984b. *The next ten years: public expenditure and taxation into the 1990s.* Cmnd. 9189. London: HMSO.

Treasury and Civil Service Committee. 1984. *The Government's economic policy: autumn statement.* HC 170 of session 1983-84. London: HMSO.

TUC. 1979. *Report of the 111th Trades Union Congress.* London: TUC.

___. 1980. *Report of the 112th Trades Union Congress.* London: TUC.

___. 1981a. *Report of the 113th Trades Union Congress.* London: TUC.

___. 1981b. *Financing the nationalised industries.* London: TUC.

___. 1982. *Report of the 114th Trades Union Congress.* London: TUC.

___. 1983. *Report of the 115th Trades Union Congress.* London: TUC.

___ and Labour Party. 1982. 'Re-acquiring public assets', in TUC 1982, 274.

Tugendhat, C. 1970. Defining a role for the state, *Financial Times,* 22 December.

Undy, R. 1978. The devolution of bargaining levels and responsibilities in the TGWU 1965-75, *Industrial Relations Journal* 9, 3, 44-56.

Webb, M. G. 1984a. Privatisation and the UK energy industries. *The Economic Review* 1, 1-5.

___. 1984b. Energy policy and privatisation of UK energy industries, *Energy Policy* (forthcoming).

Weiner, H. E. 1960. *British labour and public ownership.* London: Stevens.

Winchester, D. 1983. 'Industrial relations in the public sector', in G. S. Bain (ed.) *Industrial relations in Britain.* Oxford: Blackwell.

Zabalza, A. 1984. *Comment on Foster, Henry and Trinder, 1984.* Working paper no. 611, London: Centre for Labour Economics, London School of Economics.